United Nations Economic Commission for Europe
Food and Agriculture Organization
of the United Nations

Timber Section,
Geneva, Switzerland

Geneva Timber and Forest Discussion Papers

FORESTRY COOPERATION WITH COUNTRIES IN TRANSITION

Status report 2002, prepared in accordance with MCPFE Resolution H3

"Cooperation with Countries with Economies in Transition"

by Dr. Peter Csoka
for UNECE/FAO, Geneva

UNITED NATIONS

New York and Geneva, 2003

Note

The designations employed and the presentation of material in this publication do not imply the expression of any opinion whatsoever on the part of the secretariat of the United Nations concerning the legal status of any country, territory, city or area, or of its authorities, or concerning the delimitation of its frontiers or boundaries.

Abstract

This paper contains information supplied by national correspondents, in accordance with the commitments in resolution H3 of the 1993 Ministerial Conference on the Protection of Forests in Europe (MCPFE), on forestry assistance to countries with economies in transition. There is information on more than 650 individual projects as well as information on user needs and some analysis of the type of cooperation being used. The H3 database will be posted on the Timber Committee website (http://www.unece.org/trade/timber/h3/h3.htm). Comments, suggestions and further information are welcome. Please send them to info.timber@unece.org

ECE/TIM/DP/28

UNITED NATIONS PUBLICATIONS

Sales No. E.03.II.E.29

ISBN 92-1-116844-9
ISSN 1020 7228

UNECE/FAO TIMBER AND FOREST DISCUSSION PAPERS

The objective of the Discussion Papers is to make available to a wider audience work carried out, usually by national experts (consultants), in the course of UNECE/FAO activities. They do not represent the final official output of the activity, but rather a contribution, which because of its subject matter, or quality, or for other reasons, deserves to be disseminated more widely than the restricted official circles from whose work it emerged, or which is not suitable (e.g. because of technical content, narrow focus, specialised audience) for distribution in the UNECE/FAO *Timber and Forest Study Paper* series.

In all cases, the author(s) of the discussion paper are identified, and the paper is solely their responsibility. The UNECE Timber Committee, the FAO European Forestry Commission, the governments of the authors' country and the UNECE/FAO secretariat, are neither responsible for the opinions expressed, nor the facts presented, nor the conclusions and recommendations in the discussion paper.

In the interests of economy, *Discussion Papers* are issued in the original language only. They are available on the Timber Committee website, http://www.unece.org/trade/timber, and upon request from the secretariat. They are distributed automatically to nominated forestry libraries and information centres in member countries. Those interested in receiving these Discussion Papers on the continuing basis should contact the secretariat.

Another objective of the *Discussion Papers* is to stimulate dialogue and contacts among specialists. Comments or questions should be sent to the secretariat, who will transmit them to the authors.

Preface

The Second Ministerial Conference on the Protection of Forests in Europe, held in 1993, adopted four resolutions. Resolution H3 concerns *Forestry assistance to countries with economies in transition*, wherein signatory countries and the European Union made a number of commitments in this respect. The mandate to coordinate follow-up and monitoring of resolution H3 was entrusted to UNECE/FAO in Geneva. This discussion paper contains the second interim report on the implementation of resolution H3, consisting of the information supplied by signatory countries and stored in a database in Geneva, which now contains information on more than 650 projects. This report contains a list of the projects as well as an overview of the pattern of assistance.

This report will serve as the basis for a report to be submitted to the next Ministerial Conference on the Protection of Forests in Europe, at Vienna in April 2003. Our organisations are proud to continue to contribute, through monitoring and analysis to the pan European effort to assist the countries in transition, and intend to continue this contribution also in the future.

M. Hosny El-Lakany
Assistant Director-General, FAO
Forestry Department

Brigita Schmögnerová
Executive Secretary
UN Economic Commission for Europe

Table of contents

List of Acronyms

CIS:	Commonwealth of Independent States.
CITs:	Countries with economies in transition.
COFO:	Committee on Forestry (FAO).
C&I:	Criteria and Indicators (for sustainable forest management).
EBRD:	European Bank for Reconstruction and Development.
EFC:	European Forestry Commission (FAO).
EFI:	European Forest Institute.
EU:	European Union.
EUFORGEN:	European Forest Genetic Resources Programme.
FAO:	Food and Agriculture Organization of the United Nations.
FRA:	Forest Resources Assessment.
GEF:	Global Environment Facility.
ICP Forests:	International Cooperative Programme on the Monitoring and Assessment of Air Pollution Effects on Forests.
IFF:	Intergovernmental Forum on Forests.
IPF:	Intergovernmental Panel on Forests.
IPGRI:	International Plant Genetic Resources Institute.
IUFRO:	International Union of Forest Research Organizations.
LIFE:	l'instrument financier pour l'environnement (EU financial instrument for the environmental protection).
MCPFE:	Ministerial Conferences of the Protection of Forests in Europe.
NFAP:	National Forestry Action Plan.
NFP:	National Forest Programme.
NGO:	Non-governmental organization.
NIPIEIlesprom:	Scientific and Research Institute for Economics of the Forestry Sector (Russia).
Phare	EU's financial instrument for supporting CITs (originally: Polish-Hungarian Assistance in Restructuring Economies).
SFM:	Sustainable Forest Management.
SIDA:	Swedish International Development Agency.
UK:	the United Kingdom.
UN:	United Nations .
UNECE:	United Nations Economic Commission for Europe (regional office of the UN for Europe, including all countries of the former USSR and North America).
UNFF:	United Nations Forum on Forests.
UNCED:	United Nations Conference on Environment and Development.
UNDP:	United Nations Development Programme.
UNEP:	United Nations Environment Programme.
USA:	United States of America.
USAID:	US Agency for International Development.
TBFRA:	Temperate and Boreal Forest Resources Assessment. (Forest Resources of Europe, CIS, North America, Australia, Japan and New Zealand).
TFAP:	Tropical Forestry Action Plan.
ToS:	Team of Specialists.
TC:	UNECE Timber Committee.
TCP:	Technical Cooperation Programme (FAO).
WWF:	World Wild Fund for Nature.

Abbreviations of currencies:

€:	EURO
$:	United States dollar
£:	United Kingdom pound
DEM:	German Mark
CHF:	Swiss Franc
DKK:	Danish Krone
EEK:	Estonian Krone
FIM:	Finnish Mark
NOK:	Norwegian Krone
SEK:	Swedish Krone

1   Background

The UNECE Timber Committee considered establishing a special cooperation in the field of forestry with the former socialist countries for the first time in 1990, as a response to the relevant decisions by the plenary session of the UN Economic Commission for Europe. The first *ad hoc* meeting was held in Austria in 1992 to identify the needs of the countries with economies in transition (CITs)[1] and the possibilities for carrying out assistance programmes.

The Second Ministerial Conference on the Protection of Forests in Europe (MCPFE) held in 1993 in Helsinki resulted in, among others, Resolution H3 on "Forestry Cooperation with Countries with Economies in Transition ". This resolution gave a new impetus to the work in this field. The UNECE Timber Committee together with the FAO European Forestry Commission decided in 1994 to set up a team of specialists (ToS) with a mandate to periodically review the UNECE/FAO programme of assistance to CITs and make recommendations for the future.

The UNECE/FAO Timber Section was invited to act as international coordinator for the follow-up of Resolution H3 and monitoring its implementation. Since then, the assistance to CITs in the whole UNECE region has been monitored through the MCPFE process. The key tool for assisting monitoring and coordination of activities in this area is an ACCESS DATABASE, which was developed by the UNECE/FAO Timber Section with the direct input of the national H3 correspondents.

The first round of monitoring of activities aiming the implementation of Resolution H3 was completed in 1994 and presented to the 52nd session of the Timber Committee in the same year, and then to the 2nd Expert Level Follow-up Meeting of the Helsinki Ministerial Conference and the 28th session of the European Forestry Commission, both in January 1995.

Based on the decisions by these fora, a second round of monitoring was completed in 1996 and the results were presented to the 3rd Expert Level Follow-up Meeting and the joint session of the European Forestry Commission and the Timber Committee in 1996. The joint session took note of the report and agreed that the implementation of Resolution H3 should be demand driven and transparent. The countries were invited to submit information on new activities as it becomes available.

The relevant chapter of the progress report prepared for the Third Ministerial Conference (Lisbon 1998) was based on the information available from the Team of Specialists as well as from the H3 database.

The MCPFE work programme developed on the basis of the decision by the Lisbon Conference recognized the role of the Team of Specialists and the Timber Section in the implementation of Resolution H3. The mandate of the ToS was reviewed and updated in accordance with this recognition. The last meeting of the ToS was jointly organised with the MCPFE workshop on countries in transition in September 2001 in Dębe (Poland).

The current report is based on the latest information available from the H3 database, the TBFRA-2000 database and country reports prepared for the meetings of the Team of Specialist in 1999 in Gmunden, Austria and in 2001 in Dębe, Poland. The report aims to give a comprehensive picture of the major developments as well as of the condition of forests of the CITs region with a view to contributing to the preparations for the forthcoming Fourth Ministerial Conference in 2003 in Austria.

_____

[1] This wording was in general use during the 1990s, and was used for the resolution of the Ministerial Conference. It is therefore used throughout this study, even though some the these countries have now completed the "transition phase".

2   Executive Summary

The forest area of the transition countries comprises about one fourth of the world's total forests. The high share of virgin and old-growth forests makes the region extremely important, not only as a source of forest goods and services, but also as a source of biological diversity.

The CITs recently went through substantial changes, completely reorganizing their economical and political system. The transition process in many countries included a change of ownership structure, and was accompanied by unfavourable environmental changes. In spite of these threats, considerable deterioration of the forest resources was avoided by most of the countries except those with the most severe social and political tension. Many countries were able to expand their forest area but symptoms such as temporal and local overexploitation, calamities, increase of unmanaged areas, economical disturbances in the private and State sector were reported by many of them.

The issue of transition got a very high recognition in the international dialogue on forests. Not only specialized agencies, such as FAO and UNECE, but also high-level political fora including UNCED, IPF, IFF and UNFF, all took note of the transition countries' specific problems. In the regional context the MCPFE devoted considerable political attention to these countries, resulting in concrete actions and intensified cooperation with and among the CITs.

The transition countries started to reform their legal and institutional framework and developed an impressive number of new policies, strategies and legal documents aiming at sustainable management of their forests. However, it should be noted that transformation and development of the economic environment of sustainable forest management is very resource demanding, and the CITs were able to produce less development in this field, partly due to the generally weak performance of their economies as a whole.

The cooperation with countries in transition remained intensive throughout the nineties, resulting in a constantly increasing number of projects. While the second report on the implementation of Resolution H3 reported 249 projects at the end of 1995, the current dataset has information on more then 650 cooperative projects. This increase is partly due to the efforts to make the dataset more complete. About 280 projects were reported in the period after 1995, and an additional 55 projects are labelled *"Ongoing"* or *"In planning"* but without reference to the period of implementation. This means that the number of known cooperation projects has doubled in the period 1996-2001.

Cooperation projects were implemented through different means, especially larger ones consisting of several elements. Most of them aimed at dissemination of knowledge, experience and information. Education and training was reported in 165 projects, workshops and seminars in 101, study tours in 104. Know-how transfer was a recognized element in 121 projects. 163 projects had a research element, and capacity building was found in 79 projects; 66 projects aimed at policy/strategy development, while technical development was a focus in 63 projects. Technical assistance was reported in 19 projects; financial assistance in 5 projects.

The overwhelming majority of the projects were implemented through bilateral cooperation, while multilateral projects represent about one fourth of all projects reported.

The analyses show certain discrepancies in the dataset. These are due to completely missing reports from some countries expected to play an important role in the cooperation with countries in transition. The other source of the problems is the incompleteness of the reports - information, such as period of implementation, status, identification of targets and partners is missing in several reports. Although all these constitute a minor portion of the information set, their absence seriously undermines the usefulness of the whole dataset.

With a little additional resources and work, the quality of the database could be improved considerably. The Timber Committee together with the European Forestry Commission as well as the MCPFE Expert Level Meeting may wish to consider proposals aimed at achieving this.

Future cooperation is expected to focus on the following issues identified by recent work of the Team of Specialists and national correspondents: economically viable, multifunctional sustainable forest management and its enabling legal and financial environment, the conservation and sustainable development of forest resources, the development of the institutional framework of the public and private forestry as well as the forestry administration, the increasing of public awareness of forest issues, involvement of the public in forestry matters and recognition of the cross-sectoral nature of most forestry issues.

There is a need to take into consideration the heterogeneity of the needs arising from the development of the last decade and make better use of experiences gained so far through intra-regional cooperation.

3 Forest resources of the transition countries

3.1 *Forest area*

Twenty-seven countries from central and eastern Europe and the former USSR are considered as countries with economies in transition, but only 9 countries constituted this region in 1989, at the beginning of the political changes. According to the TBFRA-2000[2]- the latest information available on forest resources, the geographical area of the region is approximately 2,347 million ha, of which 898 million ha is covered by forests. This is about one fourth of the world's total forested area and one half of the temperate and boreal forest area. Additionally, there is about 80 million ha of other wooded land in this region, which is less important as a source of wood, but extremely important in environmental terms.

Although often classified as one group, "countries in transition" are very heterogeneous by history, economy, and also by forest resources. While the forest cover is as high as 54.5% in Slovenia, 48.1 in Estonia, or 46.4% in Latvia, this ratio is as low as 9.8% in the Republic of Moldova. Other countries of the former USSR are also very different in this respect; the forest cover is 49.9% in the Russian Federation and only 2.8% in Tajikistan.

---

[2] UNECE/FAO: Forest Resources of Europe, CIS, North America, Australia, Japan and New Zealand

Table 1
Forest resources of the transition countries
(1,000 ha)

Country name	Period	Total	Land	Water	FOWL	Forest	OWL	Other	Population (1,000)
Albania	1995	2 875	2 759	116	1 030	1 030	0	1 729	3 119
Bosnia and Herzegovina	1995	5 120	5 073	47	2 710	2 276	434	2 363	3 675
Bulgaria	1995	11 098	10 895	202	3 903	3 590	314	6 992	8 336
Croatia	1996	5 654	5 592	62	2 105	1 775	330	3 487	4 481
Czech Republic	1995	7 887	7 728	159	2 630	2 630	0	5 098	10 282
Estonia	1996	4 523	4 187	336	2 162	2 016	146	2 025	1 429
Hungary	1996	9 303	9 093	210	1 811	1 811	0	7 282	10 116
Latvia	1997	6 459	6 222	237	2 995	2 884	111	3 227	2 424
Lithuania	1996	6 530	6 267	263	2 050	1 978	72	4 217	3 694
Poland	1992 - 96	31 268	30 435	833	8 942	8 942	0	21 493	38 718
Romania	1995 - 97	23 839	22 949	890	6 680	6 301	379	16 269	22 474
Slovakia	1996	4 903	4 810	93	2 031	2 016	15	2 779	5 377
Slovenia	1996	2 027	2 016	11	1 166	1 099	67	850	1 993
The FYR of Macedonia	1995	2 571	2 531	40	988	906	82	1 543	1 999
Yugoslavia	1995	10 217	10 112	105	3 480	2 894	586	6 632	10 635
European CITs		**134 274**	**130 671**	**3 603**	**44 683**	**42 148**	**2 535**	**85 987**	**128 752**
Armenia	1996	2 974	2 846	128	392	334	58	2 454	3 536
Azerbaijan	1988	8 642	8 342	300	990	936	54	7 352	7 669
Belarus	1994 - 97	20 760	20 285	475	8 936	7 865	1 071	11 349	10 315
Georgia	1995	6 970	6 831	139	2 988	2 988	0	3 843	5 059
Kazakhstan	1993	272 490	272 490	0	16 673	10 504	6 169	255 817	16 319
Kyrgyzstan	1995	19 850	19 700	150	797	729	68	18 903	4 643
Republic of Moldova	1997	3 385	3 309	75	355	324	31	2 954	4 378
Russian Federation	1993	1 709 761	1 637 733	72 028	886 538	816 538	70 000	751 195	147 434
Tajikistan	1995	14 310	14 270	40	730	400	330	13 540	6 015
Turkmenistan	1995	48 800	48 100	700	3 754	3 754	0	44 346	4 309
Ukraine	1996	60 355	57 936	2 419	9 494	9 458	36	48 442	50 861
Uzbekistan	1988	44 740	42 540	2 200	2 170	1 909	261	40 370	23 574
CIS		**2 213 036**	**2 134 382**	**78 654**	**933 817**	**855 739**	**78 078**	**1 200 564**	**284 112**
Total CITs		**2 347 309**	**2 265 052**	**82 257**	**978 501**	**897 888**	**80 613**	**1 286 552**	**412 864**

Source: TBFRA-2000 database

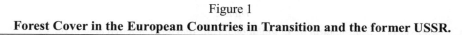

Figure 1
Forest Cover in the European Countries in Transition and the former USSR.

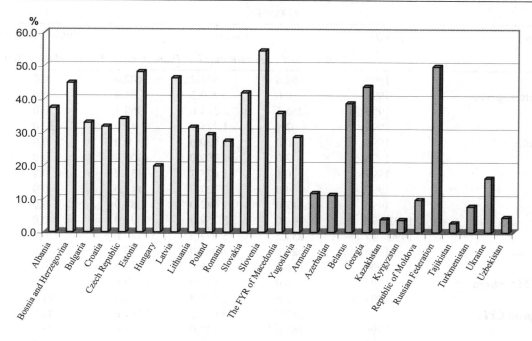

☐ European CITs

■ CIS

Source: TBFRA-2000 database

The relation between forest area and population also varies on a wide scale. The forest land per capita varies between 5.54 ha (Russian Federation) and 0.07 ha (Tajikistan and Moldova).

The importance of the forest resources of the region is determined not only by their extent but also quality. The large areas of virgin or old-growth (primarily coniferous) forests, mainly in the Russian Federation, make the region even more important on the global level, since these areas are very important gene pools and resources of biological diversity.

Table 2

Undisturbed, Semi-natural and Plantation forests and other wooded land in the CITs

(1,000 ha)

Country name	Period	Forest			Other wooded land	
		Undisturbed	*Semi-natural*	*Plantations*	*Undisturbed*	*Semi-natural*
Albania	1995	84.8	843.2	102.0	0.0	0.0
Bosnia and Herzegovina	1995	0.0	2 219.3	56.9	0.0	433.6
Bulgaria	1995	256.5	2 364.6	968.5	0.0	313.8
Croatia	1996	2.4	1 725.7	47.0	33.0	297.0
Czech Republic	1995	0.0	2 630.0	0.0	0.0	0.0
Estonia	1996	2.0	1 709.0	305.0	0.0	146.0
Hungary	1996	0.1	1 674.7	136.2	0.0	0.0
Latvia	1997	4.0	2 737.0	143.0	0.0	111.0
Lithuania	1996	12.0	1 682.0	284.0	0.0	72.0
Poland	1992 - 96	144.0	8 758.0	39.0	0.0	0.0
Romania	1990 - 97	233.2	5 977.4	90.6	0.0	0.0
Slovakia	1996	20.0	1 981.0	15.0	0.0	15.0
Slovenia	1996	50.0	1 048.0	1.0	0.0	67.0
The FYR of Macedonia	1995	0.0	876.0	30.0	0.0	82.0
Yugoslavia	1995	3.6	2 851.4	39.4	11.7	573.8
Total European CITs		812.6	39 077.2	2 257.6	44.7	2 111.2
Armenia	1996	284.0	37.0	13.0	41.0	17.0
Azerbaijan	1988	400.0	515.5	20.0	15.0	39.0
Belarus	1994 - 97	43.5	7 626.5	194.8	0.0	1 071.3
Georgia	1995	550.0	2 238.4	200.0	0.0	0.0
Kazakhstan	1993	0.0	10 499.0	5.0	0.0	6 169.0
Kyrgyzstan	1988	100.0	572.0	57.0	0.0	68.0
Republic of Moldova	1997	0.0	322.8	1.3	0.0	30.8
Russian Federation	1993	749 198.0	50 000.0	17 340.0	70 000.0	0.0
Tajikistan	1995	21.0	369.0	10.0	18.0	312.0
Turkmenistan	1995	0.0	3 742.0	12.4	0.0	0.0
Ukraine	1996	59.0	4 974.0	4 425.0	6.0	30.0
Uzbekistan	1988	200.0	1 409.0	300.0	0.0	261.0
Total CIS		**750 855.5**	**82 305.2**	**22 578.5**	**70 080.0**	**7 998.1**
Total TBFRA region (including N. America, Oceania, W. Europe)		**751 668.1**	**121 382.4**	**24 836.1**	**70 124.7**	**10 109.3**

Source: TBFRA-2000 database

The transition countries comprise about 81% of the total undisturbed forests of the TBFRA region. As far as nature conservation is concerned, about 37% of the CIT"s region's forests are in the IUCN[3] classes I -II, and 21% of the CIT's forests are in IUCN classes III - IV.

The development of the forest cover is an issue of utmost importance during the transition process, because the overall economical and social changes often have adverse effects on forests. Uncontrolled felling and overexploitation of forests are often the accompanying symptoms of economical disturbances. Many of these symptoms were observed in most of the transition countries; however, it appears from the data that the strong forestry traditions and administrative measures implemented were able to counterbalance, at least partly, the undesirable developments. Many countries were able to continue to increase their forest cover. As for the European CITs, the forest area has been increasing considerably in almost all of them over the past 50 years, reaching an impressive increase of 125% in Estonia, 110% in FYR of Macedonia, 75% in

---

[3] IUCN classes: I: Nature reserve/wilderness area, II: National park, III: Natural monument, IV: Habitat/species management area, V: Protected landscape, VI: Managed resource protection area

Lithuania, 56% in Hungary, or in absolute terms 2.3 million ha in Poland alone. The forest cover had been decreasing for decades in Albania, and contradictory information is available for Bosnia and Herzegovina on whether the forest cover is stable or slightly decreasing.

According to the TBFRA-2000, Yugoslavia reported an annual 1450 ha decrease of forest cover between 1979 and 1995. Overall though, the forest area of the European CITs increased by 85 thousand ha annually in the reference period concerned.

The forest cover is stable or increasing in the CIS countries with the exception of Russia where statistics show a considerable loss of forest cover amounting to 1.1 million ha/year. This is partly counterbalanced by an increase of other wooded land, resulting in a net growth of the wooded area in statistical terms, but the loss of forest cover may have far reaching consequences. (Unfortunately, different sources provide different explanations, from overexploitation to alternative land uses and changes in terms and definitions).

Table 3
Change of the forest cover
(1,000 ha)

Country name	Period 1	Period 2	Period 1	Period 2	Average annual change	Period 1	Period 2	Average annual change
			Forest			*Other wooded land*		
Albania	1957	1995	1 328	1 030	-7.8	0	0	0
Bosnia and Herzegovina	1990	1995	2 276	2 276	0	434	434	0
Bulgaria	1985	1995	3 386	3 590	20.4	298	314	1.6
Croatia	1986	1996	1 758	1 775	2	333	330	-0.1
Czech Republic	1986	1995	2 625	2 630	0.5	0	0	0
Estonia	1988	1996	1 916	2 016	12.5	102	146	5.5
Hungary	1990	1996	1 768	1 811	7.2	0	0	0
Latvia	1988	1997	2 757	2 884	12.7	143	111	-3.2
Lithuania	1987	1996	1 930	1 978	4.8	64	72	0.8
Poland	1987 - 91	1992 - 96	8 886	8 942	11	0	0	0
Romania	1955	1990	5 772	6 301	14.7			
Slovakia	1988	1996	1 961	2 016	6.9	15	15	0
Slovenia	1986	1996	1 077	1 099	2.2	67	67	0
The FYR of Macedonia	1990	1995	906	906	0	82		
Yugoslavia	1979	1995	2 918	2 894	-1.4	586		
European CITs			**41 264**	**42 148**	**85.6**	**1 455**	**2 156**	**4.6**
Armenia	1983	1996	292	334	4.2	35	58	2.3
Azerbaijan	1983	1988	870	936	13	52	54	0.4
Belarus	1988	1994	6 327	7 865	256.2	857	1 071	35.6
Georgia	1990	1995	2 988	2 988	0	0	0	0
Kazakhstan	1988	1993	9 310	10 504	239	5 787	6 169	76
Kyrgyzstan	1988	1993	729	843	22.8	68	68	0
Republic of Moldova	1988	1997	318	324	0.6	31	31	0
Russian Federation	1988	1993	821 988	816 538	-1 090.00	62 105	70 000	1 579.00
Tajikistan	1988	1995	386	400	2	330	330	0
Turkmenistan	1990	1995	3 754	3 754	0	0	0	0
Ukraine	1988	1996	9 213	9 458	31	35	36	0.1
Uzbekistan	1988	1995	1 909	1 946	4.6	261		
CIS			**858 085**	**855 890**	**-516.6**	**69 561**	**77 817**	**1 693.40**
Total CITs			**899 349**	**898 038**	**-431**	**71 016**	**79 973**	**1 698.00**

Source: TBFRA-2000 database

3.2 *Growing stock and increment*

The region is characterized by a large variety of site and climatic conditions reflected by the growing stock values as well. The forests of the European CITs have 7.8 billion m³ of the approximately 25 billion m³ of European growing stock, ranging from 70 m³/ha in FYR of Macedonia to 282.6 m³/ha in Slovenia and averaging 179.5 m³/ha in the region. The countries of the former USSR have 89.5 billion m³ of growing stock of which 85.5 billion m³ is in Russia. Different stand types and structures are reflected by the relatively low volume of 104.5 m³/ha in Russia, 145.2 m³/ha in Georgia (the highest value in the region), and 3.8 m³/ha in Turkmenistan (the lowest).

The net annual increment reflects the same heterogeneity ranging from 1 m³/ha/year in Albania to 7.9 m³/ha/year in the Czech Republic, with an average of 4.1 m³/ha/year for the European CITs, while this value is very low in the former USSR, with 1.5 m³/ha/year in Azerbaijan and 1.2 m³/ha/year in Russia.

The felling intensity expressed in per cent of the increment varied between 83% (Albania, Czech Republic) and 36% (Slovenia) and was well below the 70% European average for the whole region

Not only the intensity of felling changed in this period, but its composition as well, as regards the proportion of felling from losses. This unplanned felling seems to be a long-term problem in areas with high air pollution, potentials for high winds, snow and frost (Czech Republic, Slovakia, Poland, Romania, Slovenia). In other regions such as the Baltics, biotic agents, pests and diseases appear to be the causes, while in the southeastern countries; fires are identified as main reasons.

While the volume of wood coming from sustainably managed forests decreased considerably, there were other factors, which have increased the exploitation of the forests in an undesired way. The collapse of the traditional domestic and international markets for agricultural products caused serious problems for a high proportion of the population. This, together with the high energy-prices led to an increase of illegal felling, primarily for local use. In addition to these problems a number of new forest owners were doubtful about the long-term nature of the changes, so they wanted to make money from their new properties as soon as possible by harvesting and selling wood, and were not too much concerned with sustainability. These illegal activities did not threaten with exceeding the volume limits of harvesting set by the current increment, but could cause serious local problems by overexploiting certain areas, hindering regeneration, giving way to site deterioration, erosion, and unfavourable changes of the water regime.

A study[4] on the forest sector of the Phare countries, based on national reports and consultations with national correspondents, considered the various factors affecting the forest sector of the countries concerned, and summarised the current state and future development of felling as follows:

Table 4

Facts and forecasts about felling in selected CITs

(+increase; - decrease; +- fluctuate; 0 no change)

	Date/trend	AL	BA	BG	CZ	EE	HU	LA	LT	MK	PL	RO	SK	SI
Felling Intensity %	mid 1990s	83	52	40	83	52	60	51	54	61	74	39	53	36
Felling of losses and illegal felling	Period	1994	1990	1990	90-96	1995	1996	1996	91-96	1995	1996	90-96	90-96	1996
	% of felling	40	16	16	60	8	12	21	30	13	36	30	53	47
Total felling	Short term	+	0	-	0	+	-	+	+	0	+	0	-	-
	Long term	+	+	+	+	+	0	0	+	+	+	0	0	+
Felling of losses	Short term	+-	+		0	+	0	0	+	+-	0	+	+	+
	Long term	-	+		+	+	+	+	+-	+-	+	0	+	
Source: see footnote														

---

[4] Phare Programme: Conservation and Sustainable Management of Forests in Central and Eastern European Countries, 1999

The study drew the following conclusion on the present state and future development of felling in the 13 Phare partner countries: "*Air pollution, the growth of conifers outside their natural range, and many other intervention make the forests less stable and susceptible to diseases and pests. The synergy of these factors reduces the life expectations of forest tree species especially in Central Europe, where growing stocks are the highest in Europe, and rotation ages of Norway spruce and Scots pine, for example, are found to be longer than in southern Finland. As a consequence, not only air pollution but also the practice of retaining forests which are biologically too old contributes to inferior forest condition in the region.*" (Longauer, 1999)

4 Development of the legal framework

The transition process was characterised by very similar symptoms in the whole CIT region. The forestry sector found itself in a very complicated situation, as it had to conserve its multifunctional character and at the same time, adapt itself to a new economical environment, policy and legal framework. This included: changing of ownerships of forest land through privatisation and restitution processes, keeping and enlarging employment possibilities in rural areas responding to the challenge of agricultural over-production, providing a sufficient amount of wood for industry while maintaining environmental and social services to the public, and conservation of biological diversity and forest ecosystems.

Most of the European CITs decided to re-establish private ownership through restitution in several fields, including forestry, while the countries of the CIS kept their forests completely in the public domain. The prevailing State forestry companies and the large forestry complexes were split up and reorganised. Traditional silviculture was very often separated from forest industries in technical and legal terms.

As a response to all these transition problems and to the ongoing international developments, forestry had to develop a legal and economical environment suitable for sustainable development of forest resources and forest industries. This included building capacities to support the emerging private sector, restructuring the State forestry and improving environmental consciousness and public participation.

Table 5
Forest-related policies and legal instruments in selected CITs

ALBANIA	
The Green Strategy, 1991	Law on Forestry and the Forest Service Police, 1992
Law on Environmental Protection, 1993	Law on Pastures and Meadows, 1995
Wildlife Law, 1995	Law on Forest Revenue, 1998
Regulation on the Transfer of Forests and Pastures in Use to Communes, 1996	Law on Leasing the State Owned Agricultural Land, Meadows, Pastures and Forests, 1998
ARMENIA	
Forest Code, 1994	Forest Policy for Armenia, 196
BELARUS	
Forest Code, 2000	
Concept for sustainable development of the forestry of Belarus, 1996	Concept of Sustainable Development of Forestry up to 2015, 1997
BOSNIA AND HERZEGOVINA	
Forest Law, 1993 (revision in process)	Law on protection and use of cultural-historical and natural heritage, 1985
BULGARIA	
Law for the Forest, 1997	Law for the Restitution of Forests, 1997
Law for the Hunting, 1997	
CROATIA	
Forest Law, 1990, 1993	Law on Fire Protection, 1993
Law on Environmental Protection, 1994	Law on Plant Protection, 1994
Law on Hunting, 1994	Law on Water, 1995
Law on Forest Seed and Planting Material, 1995	National Forest Policy, 1991

Table 5 (cont.)

CZECH REPUBLIC	
Act on Inspection of the Environment and its Competence in Forest Protection	Act on the Protection of Nature and the Landscape, 1992
Act on the Environment	Principles of the State Forest Policy 1994
Forest Act, 1995	Act on Game keeping, (bill approved by Gov. in 2001)
Gov. Order on Performance of Forest Inventory in 2001-2004, 2001	
ESTONIA	
Forest Act, 1993, 1997	Forest Development Programme, 1995
Estonian Forest Policy, 1997	Development Plan for the Forest Sector 1997-2001
GEORGIA	
National Forestry Strategy, 1997	Forest Law, 1999
HUNGARY	
Afforestation programme 1985-2000	Law on Forests and the Protection of Forests 1996
Law on Nature Protection, 1996	Law on Joint Forest Tenure, 1996
Law on Hunting 1996	National Programme for Agriculture, 1
LATVIA	
Law on Forest Management and Utilisation, 1994	Law on Natural Resources Tax, 1995
National Biodiversity Action Plan, 1995	
LITHUANIA	
Forest Law, 1994, amended in 2001	Environment Protection Law, 1992, updated in 1997
Law on Protected Areas, 1993, updated in 1995	Law on Environmental Monitoring, 1997
Law on Wildlife, 1997	Law on Wild Flora, 1999
Law on Plant Protection, 1995, updated in 1998	Regulations on Forest Enterprises 1995
Reg. On General Forest Enterprise 1996	Reg. On State Forest Service 1995
Reg. On State Forest inspection 1995	Reg. On Forming and Using the Forest Fund 1995
Forestry and Forest Industry Development Programme, 1994, updated in 1996	
FYR of MACEDONIA	
Strategy for the Development of Agriculture, Forestry and Water Economy, 1995	Law on Hunting, 1996
Law on Forest, 1997	
POLAND	
Act on Forests, 1991, 1997	Act on Protection of Nature, 1991
Act on Protection of Environment, 1980, 1997	Act on Protection of Arable and Forest Land, 1995
Polish Policy for Comprehensive Forest Resource Protection, 1995	National Forest Density Advancement Programme
Land Development Law, 1994	National Policy on Forests, 1997
ROMANIA	
Law on Environmental Protection, 1995, 1999	Law on Hunting Fund and Protection of Game, 1996
Forestry Code, 1996	Law 141/1999 on diversification of forest ownership
Law 1/2000 in restitution of property right on agricultural and forest land	Gov. Decision 12/2001 on the organisation and functioning of the Ministry of Agriculture, Food and Forests
RUSSIAN FEDERATION	
Forest Code, 1997	
SLOVAKIA	
Act on the State Fund of Improvement of Forests of the Slovak Republic, 1991	Act on Forest Management and State Forestry Administration
Act on Forests, 1977	Act on the Slovak Chamber of Forestry, 1993
Conception of Forest Policy by the year 2005	
SLOVENIA	
Act on Forests, 1977	Act on the Slovenian Chamber of Forestry, 1993
Conception of Forest Policy by the year 2005	
UKRAINE	
Law on Environmental Protection, 1991	Forest Code, 1994
Law on Land, 1992	Law on Water Use, 1995
Law on Nature-Reserve Fund of Ukraine, 1992	Law on Fauna, 1993
Law on Flora, 2000	Law on Hunting Management, 2000
Moratorium on clear cutting in mountain slopes of fir-beech forests of Carpathian Region, 2000	

The development of the policy and legal framework was followed by the transformation of institutions, which was substantial in the countries where private ownership was re-established. It proved to be a difficult task because the strengths of the centrally planned system in forestry were often overestimated, while its weaknesses were underestimated. Many feared that the introduction of market conditions would threaten sustainable forest management even in the State sector.

In the course of 1992-1999 the countries with private forestry created new entities or transformed the existing ones responsible for managing the State forests. These new State entities are expected to be the shop-windows of proper forest management, and could have several special tasks, such as management of protected and recreational forests, maintenance of promotional forests, providing forestry extension and education, management of private forests on request. In some cases, they even have limited normative or authoritative roles to issue regulations (e.g. in Albania, Poland) or professionally control the management of private forests (Croatia).

Forest inventory, planning and control remained the role of the State (i.e. the forestry administration) in most of the countries. However, in the case of Albania they are merged with management activities, while in other cases, e.g. in the Czech Republic, they are privatised (except control) and operate on a contract basis.

State forestry was restructured in the countries without private forest ownership as well, but restructuring in these countries was mainly aimed at splitting up the vertical production lines and privatising certain activities.

Figure 2
Forest ownership in TBFRA 1990 and TBFRA-2000

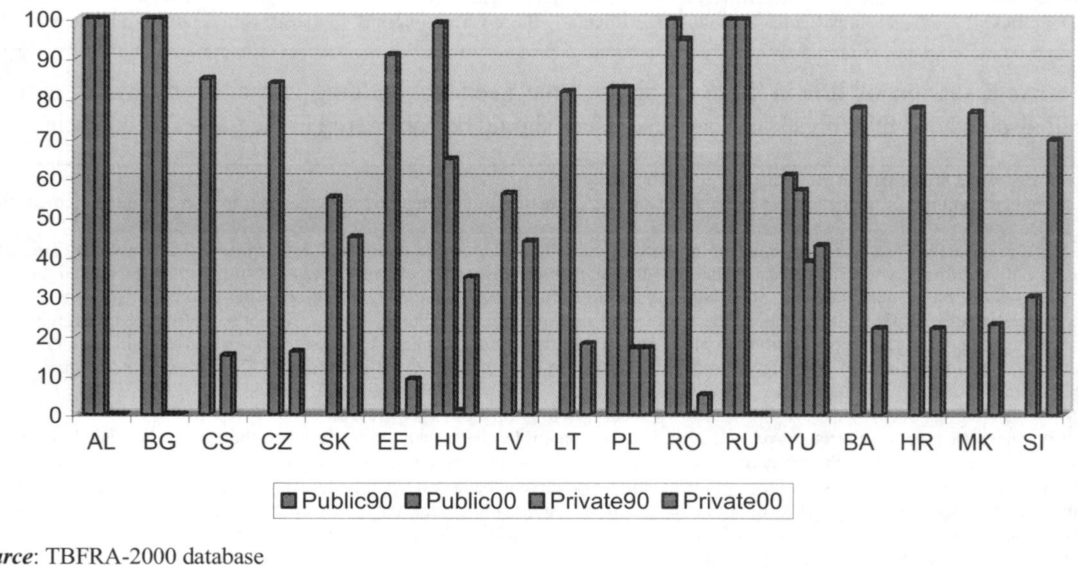

Source: TBFRA-2000 database

Privatisation in the classical sense took place only to a limited extent; the above change of forest ownership was mostly the result of the restitution process The process is not yet over: the most recent information suggests that considerable changes are expected in Bulgaria and Romania, where restitution is still in its early phase.

The complexity of the restitution process is indicated by special issues such as the property of the Church in several countries, which often required a very long time to find a satisfactory solution. Privatisation of State forests is not expected to play a decisive role in the future, but together with the foreseen afforestation on private lands, it may considerably increase the share of private forests.

5   The transition countries in the international dialogue on forests

5.1   *The IPF/IFF/UNFF process*

In 1992 the United Nations Conference on Environment and Development (UNCED) recognized the special conditions of the former socialist countries in the Forest Principles (Non-Legally Binding Authoritative Statement of Principles for a Global Consensus on the Management, Conservation and Sustainable Development of all Types of Forests).

Principles/Elements

9. (a) The efforts of developing countries to strengthen the management, conservation and sustainable development of their forest resources should be supported by the international community, taking into account the importance of redressing external indebtedness, particularly where aggravated by the net transfer of resources to developed countries, as well as the problem of achieving at least the replacement value of forests through improved market access for forest products, especially processed products. In this respect, special attention should also be given to the <u>countries undergoing the process of transition to market economies</u>

The first session of the Intergovernmental Panel on Forests in 1995 devoted special attention to environmental deterioration and recognised the CIT region as a unique region when discussing environmental deterioration globally.

I.   Implementation of the United Nations Conference on Environment and Development decisions related to forests at the national and international level, including an examination of sectoral and cross-sectoral linkages

4.   Monitor actions to support afforestation, reforestation and the restoration of forest systems, where appropriate, particularly in countries with fragile ecosystems and affected by desertification and/or drought, particularly in Africa. Within this context, also consider specific actions in countries whose forests are affected by pollution, particularly those with <u>economies in transition</u> in central and Eastern Europe

---

The second session of IPF in 1996 recognised the need for building capacities to absorb and attract finance. It also decided that forests and land use issues should be considered in the transition countries.

   A.   Programme elements that were discussed substantively
4.   International cooperation in financial assistance and technology transfer for sustainable forest management (programme element II)

44.   The Panel emphasized that existing financial resources, including ODA, should be used efficiently and effectively. This should be facilitated by policy reforms, where appropriate, that favour sustainable forest management. It was also further acknowledged that efficiency could be improved through increased absorptive capacity for financial flows in the developing countries and <u>countries with economies in transition</u>, which, in turn, might require financial support in the area of capacity-building. More efficient and effective programmes will help to attract greater financial resources. National plans and programmes for sustainable forest management should include cost-benefit considerations. The importance of transparency and a participatory approach in the elaboration of forest-related programmes were also highlighted in this context.

52.   There is a need to encourage stronger participation and investment by the private sector to attain the sustainable development of forest resources. At present, however, the objectives of the private sector do not necessarily support the promotion of sustainable forest management. While the need is recognized or formulating attractive incentives for private sector investments, enabling conditions in developing countries and <u>countries with economies in transition</u> are equally important with respect to attracting these investments. The possibility of elaborating codes of conduct applicable to forestry activities carried out through joint ventures and by the private sector, perhaps initially at the national level, was suggested in this regard.

   B.   Programme elements that were discussed initially
1.   Progress in national forest and land use plans (programme element I.1)

82.   The Panel took note of the progress report of the Secretary-General on programme element I.1 (document E/CN.17/IPF/1996/8) and requested that the following points be taken into account in preparation for substantive discussion of this issue during the third session of the Panel:

   (b)   Consideration should be given to all types of forests and utilization patterns in developing as well as developed countries, and <u>countries with economies in transition;</u>

The negotiation text of the third session of IPF contained several provisions for the CITs, identifying their special needs in:

➤ capacity building as a component of nfp,
➤ afforestation and rehabilitation of deteriorated areas,
➤ issues related to low forest cover,
➤ technology transfer and investments,
➤ cooperation with donor countries and international organisations.

The fourth IPF session in 1997 concluded in proposals for action in the fields identified by the third session.

I. IMPLEMENTATION OF FOREST-RELATED DECISIONS OF THE UNITED NATIONS CONFERENCE ON ENVIRONMENT AND DEVELOPMENT AT THE NATIONAL AND INTERNATIONAL LEVELS, INCLUDING AN EXAMINATION OF SECTORAL AND CROSS-SECTORAL LINKAGES

A. Progress through national forest programmes

17 g) Urged countries, particularly in developing countries and countries with economies in transition, to include capacity-building as an objective of national forest programmes, paying particular attention to training, extension services and technology transfer and financial assistance from developed countries, taking due account of local traditional forest-related knowledge;

B. Underlying causes of deforestation and forest degradation

31 The Panel:
(a)   Encouraged countries to undertake case studies using the diagnostic framework described above in order to:
  (i)   Identify underlying causes of deforestation and forest degradation;
  (ii)   Develop and test the usefulness of the framework as an analytical tool in assessing options for utilization of forest and forest lands;
  (iii) Refine it, disseminate the results and apply it more widely as appropriate;
(b)   Urged developed countries, the United Nations Development Programme (UNDP) and other multilateral and international organizations, including regional development banks, to assist developing countries and countries with economies in transition in those activities;

F. Needs and requirements of developing and other countries with low forest cover

58 c) Urged developed countries with low forest cover that are nevertheless endowed with suitable land and climate conditions to take positive and transparent action towards reforestation, afforestation and forest conservation, while urging other developed countries, where appropriate, notably those with low forest cover but with limited land and unsuitable climatic conditions, to assist developing countries and countries with economies in transition, in particular countries with low forest cover, to expand their forest cover, taking into account principle 8 (a) of the Forest Principles, through the provision of financial resources and transfer of appropriate technology, as well as through the exchange of information and access to technical know-how and knowledge;

(e) Urged donor countries and multilateral and international organizations to facilitate and assist developing countries and countries with economies in transition with low forest cover, where required, in building capacity for data gathering and analysis so as to enable them to monitor their forest resources.

II. INTERNATIONAL COOPERATION IN FINANCIAL ASSISTANCE AND TECHNOLOGY TRANSFER

A. Financial assistance

69 (e) Urged developed countries to formulate and create incentives, such as loan and investment guarantees, to encourage their private sector to invest in sustainable forest management in developing countries, as well as in countries with economies in transition

---

In 1997 the Intergovernmental Forum of Forests started its work. The CITs were dealt with separately in the context of NFP, implementation of the IPF proposals for action, and international cooperation under existing instruments by the second session of IFF in 1998.

Important elements for the implementation of IPF's proposals for action
9. The Forum agreed that the following are particularly important for the implementation of IPF's proposals for action:
(a) [Provision, taking into consideration the relevant chapters of Agenda 21 (see note #5) and paragraph 10 of the Non-legally Binding Authoritative Statement of Principles for a Global Consensus on the management, Conservation and Sustainable Development of All Types of Forests (Forest Principles),(see note #6) by the international donor community, international organizations and international financial institutions of new and additional resources, including through innovative mechanisms and/or measures] to mobilize finance, technical assistance and transfer of environmentally sound technology at the international and domestic levels, as well as through better use of existing mechanisms and measures, to support national forest programmes in developing countries, and countries with economies in transition, in particular countries with low forest cover and with fragile forest ecosystems;
(g) Further assistance by the international community to developing countries and countries with economies in transition in implementing the IPF's proposals for action as needed. National forest programmes could be used as a framework for channelling development assistance for implementation. Such support is particularly needed for capacity-building, and for creating participatory mechanisms and innovative financing arrangements.

F. Forest-related work of international and regional organizations and under existing instruments (programme element II.e (i) and II.e (ii))
4. The Forum acknowledged that in the context of the implementation of the IPF proposals for action, the real challenges ahead lie in further strengthening the existing partnerships among Task Force members and other international and regional organizations and instruments in respect of facilitating the establishment of new modalities of cooperation between Task Force members and other partners for making the best use of all the available forest-related institutional capabilities that exist at the regional and international levels. In this regard, through national forest programmes, special attention should be paid to supporting efforts of countries, in particular developing countries and countries with economies in transition, towards sustainable forest management."

The fourth session of IFF in 2000 made its proposals for action in the above fields and on the basis of the negotiations at the previous sessions.

9 (g) Further assistance by the international community to developing countries and countries with economies in transition in implementing the IPF proposals for action as needed. National forest programmes could be used as a framework for channelling development assistance for implementation. Such support is particularly needed for capacity-building, and for creating participatory mechanisms and innovative financing arrangements.
133. The Forum acknowledged that in the context of the implementation of the IPF proposals for action, the real challenges ahead lie in further strengthening the existing partnerships among Task Force members and other international and regional organizations and instruments in respect of facilitating the establishment of new modalities of cooperation between Task Force members and other partners for making the best use of all the available forest-related institutional capabilities that exist at the regional and international levels. In this regard, through national forest programmes, special attention should be paid to supporting efforts of countries, in particular developing countries and countries with economies in transition, towards sustainable forest management.
136. The Forum emphasized that success of the efforts being undertaken by various United Nations bodies on forest-related issues depends on addressing the economic, social and environmental components of sustainable forest management in the context of sustainable development, in a balanced manner. It was also noted that the specific conditions of developing countries and countries with economies in transition in terms of financial, technical and technological capabilities require particular attention. Inter-agency coordination should pay special attention to integrating the needs of developing countries with low forest cover in relevant policies and programmes.
143. The Forum called upon relevant international and regional organizations and instruments to consider, in their relevant policies and programmes, the needs and requirements of developing countries and countries with economies in transition, with special attention to low forest cover countries

Based on the proposal made by the fourth IFF session the United Nations Forum on Forest started its work in 2001. In its first session it accepted the Plan of Action where the need for financial and technical assistance was recognized.

Decision 1/3 Development of a plan of action for the implementation of the proposals for action of the Intergovernmental Panel on Forests/Intergovernmental Forum on Forests, which will address financial provisions
The United Nations Forum on Forests,
Stressing the importance of providing financial resources from a variety of sources, including public, private, domestic and international, as well as the importance of institutional and capacity -building in developing countries as well as countries with economies in transition in order to implement the Plan of Action,
Emphasizing the need to devise approaches to facilitate technology transfer to developing countries as well as countries with economies in transition in order to support the effective implementation of the proposals for action of the Intergovernmental Panel on Forests/Intergovernmental Forum on Forests by those countries,

1. *Decides* to adopt the Plan of Action of the United Nations Forum on Forests, contained in the annex to the present resolution, to guide the more effective and coherent implementation of the proposals for action of the Intergovernmental Panel on Forests/Intergovernmental Forum on Forests, and invites all relevant participants to work with the United Nations Forum on Forests to implement the Plan of Action;

Annex: Plan of Action of the United Nations Forum on Forests
Financial resources and other means of implementation
16. The provision of technical assistance, technology transfer, capacity-building and financial resources, in particular to developing countries as well as countries with economies in transition is essential to the implementation of the IPF/IFF proposals for action as is needed to strengthen the capacity of relevant institutions and instruments engaged in this implementation.

The second session of UNFF referred to the CITs in its Ministerial segment and in Resolution 2/3, emphasizing the need for improved cooperation in implementing the IPF/IFF proposals for action through finance, transfer of technology, capacity building, and the need to develop criteria and indicators to measure the effectiveness of the cooperation with and assistance to countries in transition.

Ministerial Declaration and Message from the United Nations Forum on Forests to the World Summit on Sustainable Development

2. We commit ourselves to the implementation of the IPF/IFF proposals for action. While recognizing that countries have the primary responsibility to implement the IPF/IFF proposals for action, we underline the importance for the international community to strengthen cooperation in the areas of finance, trade, transfer of environmentally sound technology and capacity-building, which are essential to ensure sustainable forest management in developing countries and underline countries with economies in transition. We stress the importance of national forest programmes or similar approaches, the role of criteria and indicators for sustainable forest management, and voluntary certification systems.

Resolution 2/3: Specific criteria for the review of the effectiveness of the international arrangement on forests
The United Nations Forum on Forests,

Decides that the specific criteria for the assessment of the effectiveness of the international arrangement on forests are the following:

(iv) international cooperation
· extent to which the international community, including bilateral and multilateral donors and organizations, CPF members, and international and regional processes, have facilitated the implementation of IPF/IFF proposals for action in developing countries and countries with economies in transition, inter alia, through the provision of financial, technical and scientific resources and capacity building

---

5.2 The work of FAO, UNECE and their subsidiary bodies

The continued political support from the IPF/IFF/UNFF process had a stimulating effect on the work of FAO and its subsidiary bodies. The Committee on Forestry (COFO) regularly addressed the issues of transition countries. The Committee concluded in various sessions that FAO should play an important role in policy support, monitoring of the privatization process, continued technical and financial support in implementing the IPF/IFF proposals for action, and developing national capacities for monitoring forest resources.

COFO XII 1995
33. The Committee endorsed the continued priority given by FAO to TFAP, to be expanded as the framework for NFAPs. The NFAP process was also stressed as an instrument for strategic planning, policy formulation and capacity building. Policy advice, both within and outside the NFAP framework, was a priority activity where FAO has a comparative advantage and should be used in the support of sustainable forest management. Policy support to the countries in transition to a market economy was especially commended.

COFO XIV 1999
NATIONAL FOREST POLICIES FOR SUSTAINABILITY: NATIONAL AND INTERNATIONAL CHALLENGES (ITEM 7)
27. The Committee emphasized the valuable role that the private sector can play in the forest sector and the importance of creating a suitable enabling environment for it. Some countries in Eastern and Central Europe, in transition to a market economy, stressed the value of greater market emphasis and the moves towards privatization, including restitution of forest land tenure in some countries. The Committee suggested that FAO's roles were in monitoring privatization trends and impacts and in assisting countries in their implementation.

COFO XV 2001
c) FAO support to the implementation of the Intergovernmental Panel on Forests/Intergovernmental Forum on Forests (IPF/IFF) proposals for action
The Committee:
  • requested FAO to support countries in their implementation of the IPF and IFF proposals for action, including capacity building and related technical and financial assistance especially to developing countries and countries with economies in transition, to develop and implement effective national policy frameworks and national forest programmes (para. 34).

(e) Results of the Forest Resources Assessment 2000
The Committee:
  • requested FAO to provide continued technical and financial assistance especially to developing countries and countries with economies in transition, for country capacity building in carrying out national-level assessments and monitoring, in order to improve the timely availability and quality of data (para. 51).

The Forestry Department of FAO developed its own strategy defining the future role of the Organization in forestry and the actions to be taken. In this document FAO's role in assisting the transition countries in developing their nfp schemes is identified. In the vision for the future, FAO sees a dynamically evolving SFM worldwide, attracting investment to an increasing degree, especially in certain regions such as that of the transition countries.

FAO Strategic Plan for Forestry

(b) Strengthen national forest policies
41. FAO will continue to coordinate action to facilitate the formulation, implementation and monitoring of national forest programmes (nfps) including assistance in policy development and strategic planning, and in cross-sectoral and land-use planning. Special emphasis will be given to:
assisting developing countries including SIDS, and countries with economies in transition;
developing policy and planning capacity, with particular reference to integrated land-use planning and the role of forestry in food security;
creating an investment climate that will attract the necessary financial resources to implement nfps.

V. VISION FOR THE FUTURE
62. The scenario to aim for is an increase in the area of sustainably managed forests, a slowing of the rate of deforestation in the tropics, a decrease in forest degradation world-wide and an increase in the global area of trees and forests through afforestation and reforestation especially of degraded land. The location, extent, composition, health and value of many of the goods and services represented by forest ecosystems and trees in the landscape will be more accurately known. Informed and constructive debate between a wide range of interest groups will be increasingly used to develop consensus on forest management, particularly in defining sustainable forest management and in striking a balance between environmental and developmental objectives. Policy changes will help to remove restrictions on forestry development, will promote participatory approaches towards their management, and will encourage the equitable distribution of benefits. The role of trees and forests in contributing to food security (including the wood energy required or cooking food) and environmental protection will be enhanced and better recognised. More forests will be under controlled management and periodic assessments of indicators will show a trend towards long-term sustainability. There will be a greatly increased flow of investment into the sector, particularly in developing countries and countries with economies in transition.

5.2.1 The joint work of the FAO European Forestry Commission and the UNECE Timber Committee

The cooperation with and assistance to the transition countries has been a very high priority in the programme of work of the two organisations since the early nineties. During the last joint meeting in 2000 they considered the activities implemented so far and decided on future actions. The meeting concluded that a team of specialists should guide the work, focusing on institution building in the broad sense and development of ecologically sound and market-oriented forest management.

22. The joint session noted that assistance was needed for countries with economies in transition (CIT) to participate in global processes in particular, and proposed, for example, that inter-sessional meetings could be held in countries in transition.

➢ Countries in transition
48. The joint session was informed of the activities of the UN-ECE/FAO team of specialists to monitor and develop assistance to countries of central and eastern Europe in transition in the forest and forest products sector (ToS on CITs), and the current strategic directions of this work. The joint session noted and commended the close co-operation on CITs between ECE/FAO and the Ministerial Conference on the Protection of Forests in Europe especially in monitoring the implementation of Resolution H3.
49. Participating countries expressed their appreciation of the work done so far in this priority area, and confirmed their support for the future activities of the team of specialists. The future directions, scope, quality and effectiveness of the work with countries in transitions depend on the resources to be allocated, and the joint session urged countries to consider contributing resources to this work.

A. **CORE PROGRAMME: MONITORING AND ANALYSIS OF SUSTAINABLE DEVELOPMENT OF THE FOREST AND FOREST PRODUCTS SECTOR IN THE REGION**
1.4 **Activities for countries in transition, including coordination of implementation of resolution H3 of the Helsinki Ministerial Conference**
Description: The Committee and Commission will provide assistance to the countries in transition, in order to promote the process of economic reform and transition to a market economy in their forest and forest products sector. The topics and themes to be included in this programme shall be in line with the priorities and needs identified by the countries concerned. The Committee and the Commission will contribute to implementing resolution H3 on forestry assistance to countries in transition, by monitoring and analysing this assistance; in particular to determine whether it corresponds to countries' real needs and priorities.
Method of work: The work is guided by a team of specialists, which meets regularly. The secretariat, as international coordinator for H3, collects, stores and analyses information and reports regularly to the parent bodies and, as appropriate, to meetings of the pan European process. A data base on forestry assistance to countries in transition is maintained and its contents made available. The Committee and Commission implement a wide range of activities, notably workshops, which are scheduled and organized in a flexible manner, under two broad headings:
- Institution building, including legal and policy infrastructure;
- Development of market oriented and ecologically sound enterprises.
Duration: to 2004
Outputs in 2000/2001: a workshop on sustainable development of marketing of wood and non-wood forest products and recreation services in forests. The database on forestry assistance to countries in transition, established under resolution H3 will be updated regularly and made widely available. The team will meet in 2001.

Due to the complexity of the issues the joint session was not able to come to a conclusion on the integrated programme of work for 2001-2004, and authorised the bureaux to further consider the programme elements and prepare a proposal for the forthcoming meetings of both organisations. The proposal, accepted by the Timber Committee in 2001 identified the problem of transition countries in four different areas, notably markets and statistics, forest resources assessment, European forest sector outlook studies, and policy and cross-sectoral issues (the latter includes monitoring forestry assistance to the CITs). Special attention should be paid to the CITs in terms of monitoring developments and implementing special actions, such as case studies, analyses etc.

The work programme fully considers the extended mandate of the Team of Specialists (ToS) on Countries in Transition and provides opportunity for intense regional cooperation and cooperation with other initiatives, notably the Ministerial Conferences of the Protection of Forests in Europe (MCPFE).

**UNECE TIMBER COMMITTEE AND FAO EUROPEAN FORESTRY COMMISSION
INTEGRATED PROGRAMME OF WORK, 2001-2004**

WORK AREA 1: MARKETS AND STATISTICS
Objective: Collect, analyse and disseminate information on forest products markets and forest fires in cooperation with partners in international organizations and countries. Provide fora for discussion of forest products marketing, especially in countries in transition, and on market developments and disseminate current, neutral information in order to support sustainable development in the forest products sector.
Guidance: Joint FAO/ECE Working Party on Forest Economics and Statistics
Programme elements:
1.1   Statistics on production, trade and prices of forest products
1.2   Analysis of markets for forest products
1.3   Capacity building for forest products marketing in <u>countries in transition</u>
1.4   Monitoring of markets for certified forest products
1.5   Statistics on forest fires
1.6   Information network, activities of team of specialists

Work Area 2: FOREST RESOURCE ASSESSMENT
Objective: Collect and make available the best possible data on the forests of the industrialised countries (ECE region, plus Australia, New Zealand and Japan). All activities will be carried out in close cooperation with the FAO global forest resource assessment programme (Global FRA).

Guidance: Joint FAO/ECE Working Party on Forest Economics and Statistics
Programme elements:
2.1   Collection and validation of data on forest resources, including methodological development
2.2   Main regional reports
2.3   Indicators of sustainable forest management: improve concepts, supply data
2.4   Contribution to global FRA
2.5   Country profiles of <u>countries in transition</u>
2.6   Special studies (biodiversity, forest condition, carbon flows etc.)
2.7   Information network, work area administration

Work Area 3: EUROPEAN FOREST SECTOR OUTLOOK STUDIES
Objective: Analyse the developments and outlook for the forest and forest industry sector, considering challenges and uncertainties of varying policies, market developments and the influence of exogenous factors. This should encompass all main kinds of forestry land use and all stages of forest product use, from the forest to the final consumer. The aim is to assist policy formulation and investment decision-making. The main target groups of EFSOS are policy makers, entrepreneurs, the academic community of the forest and forest products sector and the public.
Guidance: Joint FAO/ECE Working Party on Forest Economics and Statistics
Programme elements:
3.1   Outlook for European forest products markets
3.2   Outlook for European forest resources
3.3   Analysis of long-term historical driving forces
3.4   Case studies for <u>countries in transition</u>
3.5   Policy scenarios
3.6   Information network, public relations of EFSOS, fund raising

Work Area 5: POLICY AND CROSS-SECTORAL ISSUES
Objective: Monitor developments in policies and forest sector institutions, and carry out policy analysis of topics identified as important. To contribute as appropriate to the regional and global dialogue on sustainable development of the sector. Particular attention will be paid to issues of importance to countries in transition.
Guidance: Timber Committee and European Forestry Commission
Programme elements:
5.1   Contribution to and co-ordination of activities with the Ministerial Conference on the Protection of Forests in Europe
5.2   Contribution to global dialogue on forests through regional bodies such as the EFC and the MCPFE.
5.3   Monitoring changes in policies and institutions
5.4   Monitoring forestry assistance to <u>countries in transition</u> (monitoring of activities under resolution H3)
5.5   Trade and environment issues relevant to the forestry and forest products sector
5.6   Policy analysis
5.7   Forest Communicators Network
5.8   Promoting sustainable use of wood and other forest products and services
5.9   Policy issues in countries in transition, including capacity building

5.2.2 The Team of Specialists to monitor and develop assistance to countries of central and eastern Europe in transition in the forest and forest products sector

The Timber Committee together with the FAO European Forestry Commission (EFC) decided in 1993 to set up a team of specialists with a mandate to periodically review and make recommendations concerning the ECE/FAO programme of assistance to CITs. The team's mandate was approved by the 52nd session of the Timber Committee. Since then, the Team's mandate was extended twice; the most recent decision was adopted by the joint session in 2000, Rome (TIM/2000/7).

When the ECE/FAO Timber Section was designated to act as international coordinator for the follow-up of Resolution H3, the mandate of the ToS and the Timber Section work programme were modified accordingly. Since then, the assistance to CITs in the whole UNECE region has been implemented in close cooperation with MCPFE, giving an excellent example of inter-regional cooperation of countries and organisations.

The ToS during its meetings in Ljubljana (1997), Gmunden (1999) and Dębe, (2001) overviewed implementation of activities and emerging needs. On this basis, it prepared recommendations, which were submitted to its parent bodies and to the General Coordinating Committee of MCPFE.

These meetings recognised the dynamic nature of the transition process and underlined the importance of setting priorities within the countries involved, according to the evolving requirements. They also noted that countries should be clustered according to their needs, and inter- and intra-regional cooperation should benefit from such clustering. The ToS expressed the opinion that institutional and capacity building, development of a market oriented and ecologically sound forest management, as well as protection and conservation of the forest resources were of paramount importance, and cooperation should contribute to achieving this.

The ToS concluded that the H3 database was a useful tool for monitoring the process and proposed to develop and maintain it further and to make it available on the Internet. The ToS requested the Timber Section secretariat to allocate sufficient resources for providing continuous input to this work. As a result of these recommendations the database is now available on the web page in the Timber Section website at:

http://www.unece.org/trade/timber/h3/h3.htm

The Team's last two meetings brought new elements to the work. This was due to the fact that the 1999 meeting in Gmunden received considerable support from the Austrian government and the 2001 meeting in Dębe from several countries. This allowed the representation of a number of countries from the region (Armenia, Azerbaijan, Georgia, Macedonia), whose previous participation in the process was quite limited. The Team's last meeting was adjacent to a workshop organised within the MCPFE context.

5.3   The MCPFE process

Increasing concern about the condition of forests and the recognition of the environmental values of the forest resulted in concerted actions in Europe, notably the series of ministerial conferences on the protection of forests. The strong commitment of the central and eastern European countries to fight against unfavourable environmental changes was illustrated by their participation at the first Ministerial Conference held in Strasbourg in 1990. The Conference coincided with the political changes in some of the central and eastern European countries, while in others the transition process was only in a primordial stage. This fact did not prevent any of them signing the six resolutions aimed at different aspects of the protection of the European forests.

This strong commitment of the CITs prevailed through the evolution of the MCPFE process, even when its attention turned to more complex issues of sustainable forest management and its socio-economical aspects.

Table 6

Signatory CITs to the Resolutions of the Ministerial Conferences on the Protection of Forest in Europe

	S1	S2	S3	S4	S5	S6	H1	H2	H3	H4	L1	L2
Albania	+	+	+	+	+	+	+	+	+	+	+	+
Belarus							+	+	+	+	+	+
Bulgaria	>	+	+	+	>	+	+	+	+	+	+	+
Croatia											+	+
Czechoslovakia	+	+		+	+	+						
Czech Republic							+	+	+	+	+	+
Estonia							+	+	+	+	+	+
Hungary	+	+	>	+	+	+	+	+	+	+	+	+
Latvia							+	+	+	+	+	+
Lithuania							+	+	+	+	+	+
Poland	+	+	+	+	+	+	+	+	+	+	+	+
FYR of Macedonia												
Romania	+	+	+	+	+	+	+	+	+	+	+	+
Russian Fed.							+	+	+	+	+	+
Slovakia							+	+	+	+	+	+
Slovenia							+	+	+	+	+	+
Soviet Union	+	+	+	+	+	+						
Ukraine							+	+	+	+	+	+
Yugoslavia	+	+	+	+	+	+						

>   Signed later

     Existed as federal partner of another country

     Cease to exist

     Same name refers to a changed territory

The problems specific to the transition countries were not in the focus of the first conference in 1990, but the forthcoming conferences devoted much attention to this issue. The General Declaration in Helsinki stated that:

"*The Signatory States and the European Community,*

G. Aware of the limited resources currently available to combat the decline of forests and forest lands and to implement sustainable forest management in European countries with economies in transition,

declare their intention to:

2. Stimulate and promote cooperation and, if necessary, coordination of actions facilitating the adjustment of the forestry sectors in those European countries with economies in transition,"

In addition to this, the whole Resolution H3 was devoted to the cooperation with these countries providing a strong political support to the work. The resolution recognized the role of the countries and their forest resources in a European and global contexts, defined general guidelines and determined future actions.

This political commitment resulted in increased cooperation with the ongoing work within UNECE/FAO. The Programme of Work defined by clause 5 of the General Declaration of the Lisbon Conference recognized Resolution H3 as a key element of the MCPFE process and the cooperation with the UNECE/FAO as a substantial tool for its implementation. It was also decided that MCPFE would co-organize a workshop before the next ministerial conference.

The Programme of Work of the MCPFE

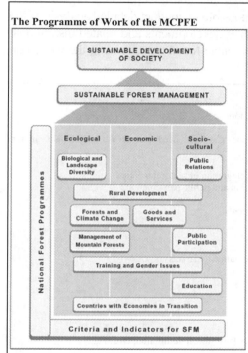

2.4 Countries in Transition (CITs)

By adopting Resolution H3 at the 2nd Ministerial Conference, the ministers committed themselves to "promote and support co-operation for mutual benefits" through a number of specific actions "in order to provide relevant expertise and advice, and to invite appropriate organisations and institutions to do likewise." They concluded "such cooperation may take the form of transfer of knowledge, and of bilateral and multilateral projects, and should focus on technical, scientific, institutional and legal matters" (Part 1: General Guidelines - 3)

Since the Helsinki Conference in 1993, the participating countries of the MPCFE have contributed to the implementation of Resolution H3 by a large number of bilateral and multilateral actions and projects, covering a wide range of forestry issues (including study tours, workshops, training projects, research programmes, technical development, know-how transfer and others).

UNECE/FAO, as international co-ordinator for Resolution H3, has developed an H3- Access Database as a tool for monitoring and co-ordination of activities in this area. This database contains information on about 500 projects of assistance and co-operation reported by donor and recipient countries and organisations. Furthermore, UNECE/FAO contributed to the implementation of the Resolution H3 through a number of other activities, notably the organisation of workshops.

The participants of the 1st ELM highlighted the efforts undertaken in the implementation of Resolution H3 and encouraged further efforts in this area. It was stated that, since the adoption of Resolution H3 in 1993, CITs have experienced diverse developments regarding forestry, which should be taken into consideration in further work of the MCPFE in this area. It was decided to support and facilitate an exchange of
- information,
- experiences and major concerns among CITs.

Work of the MCPFE

Taking into account the commitments made at past Ministerial Conferences and the decisions taken at the 1st ELM, the MCPFE will continue to support the efforts and activities undertaken by UNECE/FAO and other initiatives aiming at the promotion and support of co-operation with CITs. Furthermore, the MCPFE will co-operate in the organisation of a workshop to facilitate an exchange of information, experiences and major concerns among CITs. Poland has offered to host the workshop, which will presumably be convened in 2001.

	Actions	Actors	Time frame	Status by 10/99	Reso-lution
2.4.Countries in Transition	• Continuation of activities on forestry assistance to CITs, notably further development of H3 Access Database on Assistance Projects	UN-ECE/FAO		Ongoing	H3
	• Workshop to facilitate an exchange of information, experiences and major concerns among countries in transition to market economies	Poland in co-operation with UN-ECE/FAO and the Liaison Unit Vienna	2001	Planned	H3

It should be stated that Resolution H3 and its follow-up work have been the most decisive tools in facilitating and streamlining assistance to forestry in the CITs, and resulted in unprecedented regional cooperation and effort to achieve commonly set targets.

5.4 The International Workshop "Forests and Forestry in Central and Eastern European Countries – the Transition Process and Challenges Ahead", Debe, Poland, September 2002

The workshop was attended by 86 participants from international and non-governmental organizations, representing all European regions. This wide participation made it possible to conduct detailed analysis of the relevant issues. Based on discussions in work groups on forest policy developments and related institutional changes in the CITs, as well as on future challenges to ensure sustainable forest management, the workshop formulated a set of recommendations to be considered by the MCPFE.

I. General
• Provide forum to exchange views and experiences and to monitor progress made
• Highlight issues and priorities, including the balance of private and public interest in forests
• Provide link between global and national/regional levels
• Initiate national consultation processes to achieve integrated views of countries on issues and future needs prior to 4th Ministerial Conference

II. Policy Formulation and Implementation
• Recognize cross-sectoral nature of sustainable forest management and contribute to integration of sectoral policies
• Reinforce political commitment to promote transparency, multi-stakeholder cooperation and public participation
• Promote national forest programmes
• Reinforce implementation of existing MCPFE resolutions and international commitments

III. Economic aspects
• Promote review of fiscal systems and re-investment of forest revenues
• Enhance linkage of forestry with other forest sectors and support integration into international markets

IV. Social aspects
• Enhance human resource development and capacity building, health and safety
• Enhance communication with the public

V. Ecological aspects
• Identify urgent needs in the protection of ecological values in regions of acute stresses (war, forest destruction, erosion,...)
• Consider implications of privatization and restitution of areas rich in biodiversity
• Identify mechanisms for sustained long-term financing of ecological functions, including innovative mechanisms

---

Although the recommendations were addressed primarily to MCPFE, UNECE/FAO should also make use of them through implementation in the integrated programme of work as well.

The details on the main findings and recommendations of the workshop are presented below.

Excerpts from the Minutes of the International Workshop

"FORESTS AND FORESTRY IN CENTRAL AND EASTERN EUROPEAN COUNTRIES – THE TRANSITION PROCESS AND CHALLENGES AHEAD"

12 – 14 September 2001, Dębe, Poland

Findings of working group 1 – Socio-economic dimension of sustainable forest management

1. Transition process

Challenges identified:

- Role of government in privatisation / restitution
- Institutional and political reforms
- Reform of State forest administration
- Adaptation of legislation, including duties between national and local levels
- Unbalanced (industry) structures in forest sector

Lessons learned:

- Internal initiation, build up of expertise and lead, subsequent external support
- Co-ordination with other sectors, environmental protection policy, national situation
- Change in the right direction is possible
- Transition processes of countries and their forest sector have different scope and speed
- Participatory approach is key
- Real political will is necessary
- There is no single model that fits all countries
- Use experience made in other sectors and regions/countries
- Different importance of forest sector influences process
- Insufficient communication and information creates problems

2. Policy formulation

Challenges identified:

- Rights and duties of public and private owners
- Participation, conflict resolution, but low public interest
- Formulation and implementation of national forest programmes
- Deforestation and afforestation issues
- Cross-sectoral activities and issues

Lessons learned:

- Agricultural land changes to be faced

- Integration of forestry and rural development needed

- Reform within macro-economic framework necessary

- National forest policy is important

- Involvement of all stakeholders for policy formulation

- Communication, information and transparency

- Support of private associations

- Role of forestry for and demand of the public

- Base on local experience and international knowledge

- Follow up instruments for revision of policies to integrate implementation experience

- Co-ordinated policies between forestry and forest industry sector

3. Policy implementation and instruments

Challenges identified:

- Law enforcement, including illegal logging and corruption

- Financing SFM

- Communication and information tools

- Institutions, including support and extension

Lessons learned

- Adequate instruments needed to implement policies formulated

- Clear definitions of tasks and functions is key

- Criteria for evaluation of implementation and instruments

- Holistic approach and cross-sectoral linkages important

- Low level of law enforcement has to be addressed

- Economic, market and fiscal reform/adaptation is necessary to succeed

- General favourable investment climate facilitates investment in forestry

- Forest management can be economically balanced

- Low political and public attention,

- Currently mainly/only external international financial support

- Possibly financial potential exists from „Kyoto forests"

- Step by step implementation in the right order (starting from political will, formulation processes, law decision, implementation, extension)

- More transparency of public forest management needed

4. Market and economic aspects

Challenges identified:

- Competitiveness of forest sectors

- Changing consumption and production patterns

- Role of forestry in rural development
- Economic viability and investment promotion
- Kyoto forests and certification
- Income creation and employment, incl. through non-wood
- Management of public forests

Lessons learned:

- No excess market barriers creation / subsidising
- Develop internal resources and private structures
- Close collaboration between government and private interest groups
- Definition of appropriate relationship between public and private forest industry sector
- Efficient linkages between public and private forest industry sector
- Role of certification
- Market information
- Promotion of the use of forest products
- Consider global forest products market developments (production, consumption and market structures)
- Support innovative solutions, such as eco-tourism

5. Social aspects

Challenges identified

- Occupational safety and health
- Capacity building and human resources
- Lack of trust between stakeholders
- Public use of forests

Lessons learned:

- Capacity building is an overarching issue, investment in human resources is key
- Qualified persons might become a bottleneck
- Role of recreation services
- Dialogue between stakeholders is important
- Transparency is necessary for establishing trust
- Education and information – opening up
- Stakeholders depend on each other
- Motivate public to participate policy formulation
- Lack of studies on behaviour of private forest owners

Role of MCPFE / Ministers and Recommendations:

- Address rural development and the whole forest sector/cluster, not only forestry
- Promote participatory approach and national forest programmes
- Address instruments more specifically and recommend reinvestment of forestry revenues

Role of Team of Specialists on CITs and Recommendations:

- Collect and distribute information and experiences, including background information on policies and markets, inter alia, through market workshops

- Elaborate proposals for procedures for forest policy implementation, instruments for assessment and evaluation

- Link to policy processes and support networking between bodies

- Formulate recommendations/proposals for stronger role of MCPFE

Role of both, MCPFE and Team of Specialists on CITs, and Recommendations:

- Provide forum to exchange views and experience, monitor progress made, incl. regional workshops

- Highlight issues and priorities, including the balance of private and public interest in forests

- Ensure wide stakeholder representation and involve private forest owner representatives in policy making

- Link more strongly with forest industry sectors, support integration into international markets

- Enhance human resource development and reinforce implementation of Lisbon Resolution

- Provide link between global, national/regional levels

Findings of working group 2 – Ecological dimension of sustainable forest management

Major issues/challenges in the future:

- Restitution of areas rich in bio-diversity / Financing maintenance and/or improvement of ecological functions

- Integration of protection and management concepts

- Need for integrated planning schemes and inter-sectoral approaches based on multi-stakeholder participation - national forest programmes

- Need to invest in improving information base on forest biodiversity

- Need for education and communication

- Education of new forest owners and the public

- Communication with the public

Lessons learned in the transition process:

- Maintenance and improvement of ecological functions requires external funds and cannot be financed by the forest sector alone

- Cross-sectoral approach is needed

- Co-ordination between different instruments/institutions is essential

- Financial incentives should be based on strong government policies

- Compensation schemes exist in CEECs, but often proved to be too weak in practice

- Deeper involvement of stakeholders and increased transparency is needed in setting targets for SFM

- Tasks in maintaining and/or enhancing ecological functions that require additional resources need to be defined more clearly

- Innovative financial incentives (e.g. tax relief) should be considered

- Ecosystem approach is desirable, but more experience is needed in applying it on the ground

Restitution of areas rich in biodiversity / Financing maintenance and/or improvement of ecological functions

Role of international co-operation:

- Identify urgent needs in the protection of ecological values in regions of acute stresses

- Analyse existing EU experiences and develop models applicable in the CEECs

- Recognise role of forest owners associations in sharing of experiences and networking

- Recognise NGOs' "catalytic" role

- Establish demonstration areas and analyse and integrate the existing model forest initiatives

Implications for the 4th Ministerial Conference - Recommendations:

- Contribute to integration of sector policies

- Consider broadly legal framework for SFM

- Foster implementation of existing international commitments through an action-oriented resolution

- Identify mechanisms for long-term financing of ecological functions

Integration of protection and management concepts

Role of international co-operation:

- Exchange of experiences in measuring and monitoring biodiversity

- Building capacity in forest management planning

- Launch pilot studies on appropriate management techniques

- Improve capacity of forest owners in participating in setting management targets and identifying appropriate methods

Implications for the 4th Ministerial Conference - Recommendations:

- Foster implementation of existing international commitments through an action-oriented resolution

- Contribute to currently on-going work on further improvement of forest biodiversity related pan-European indicators

Need for education and communication

Role of international co-operation:

- Facilitate exchange of experiences gained in the transition process between countries, in particular among groups of countries characterised by different constraints

- Contribute to raising awareness on ecological functions and the sustained financial resources required for providing these functions

Implications for the 4th Ministerial Conference - Recommendation:

Reinforce political commitment to promote multi-stakeholder co-operation and public participation

6 Analysis of the H3 database: cooperation with countries with economies in transition

6.1 The H3 database

As a result of the first survey conducted in 1994, the ToS and its parent bodies were of the opinion that there was a need for continuous monitoring of the implementation of Resolution H3. Setting up of a special database was considered as the best way to store and analyze the information on the H3 projects. This database was set up in 1995 and the second survey was completed with its help. No systematic survey has been performed since then, but the countries were requested to submit data as they become available. The secretariat has been taking care of the maintenance of the database by inserting new information. The database is also available on the web at the Timber Committee's website.

At present the database contains data on about 650 projects implemented directly under Resolution H3 or other arrangements aimed at the cooperation with CITs. Most of the projects were reported by the donor community (multiple reporting may have taken place). Even though there are some limitations to the database use, it has proved to be the most complete and comprehensive dataset on cooperative projects in the field of forestry.

Figure 4
Reported number of projects by country groups.

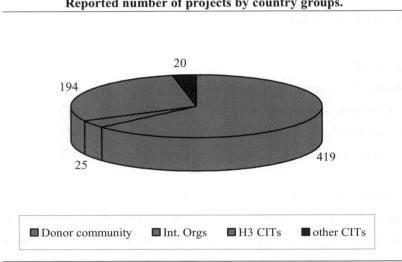

Source: H3 database

The interpretation of some of the parameters on the questionnaire/data sheet seemed to be quite difficult or diverse. There was no response provided for the reference numbers to the H3 paragraphs, the reference year (i.e. the year of reporting) is frequently missing, period of implementation does not always correspond to the status of the project, the information on finance often lacks the currency unit or is not available at all, etc. These discrepancies were, to the extent possible, corrected in the course of the evaluation, but considerable uncertainty remains.

However useful the H3 dataset is, there is a lack of internal integrity observed in some cases. It seems to be obvious that internal communication is not functioning properly and there are huge differences in and between the countries regarding the understanding of H3 projects. Even in those cases where the coordination seems to be excellent, there are alarming signs. For example: the Czech Republic reported 34 projects with Germany, and Germany reported 19 projects aimed at the Czech Republic, but none of the 53 projects is identical with any of the others. In other words, a missing country report can hardly be recovered from other countries' reports.

Another problem is that the countries are referring to the same project with different names. It is extremely difficult to find correlation between the H3 dataset and the national reports prepared (for instance) for the

Teams of Specialists' meetings. In case of absence of official titles or ID codes no comprehensive picture can be drawn by using information from different sources.

One of the ways to solve this problem could be to prepare error lists by countries and bring the errors to the attention of the respective correspondents. This would involve a relatively small amount of work in most of the countries, but such corrections could improve the quality of the dataset and thus the transparency of the whole process. As for future data input, it is desirable that incomplete or contradicting reports (records) should not be inserted in the database until the discrepancies are clarified with information providers.

These arrangement would absorb additional secretariat resources, but this should be counterbalanced by the fact that any analysis of the dataset or its use in general will be faster and more efficient as there would be no need for error checking and recovering missing data.

6.2 Activities in the countries with economies in transition

6.2.1 Signatory Countries in transition

The countries reported a total of 194 projects, but many more were retrieved from the dataset (please note that the series "total" may include multiple reporting).

Figure 5
Reported number of projects by the transition countries signatories to Resolution H3

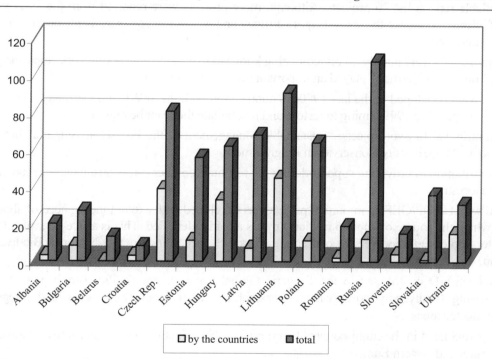

Albania

Albania reported two major projects. The first project was conducted between 1995-98 in cooperation with USAID focusing on the development of private forestry and agroforestry. The $5.3 million budget of the project financed capacity building, know-how transfer and education/training components. Austria also contributed to this project by organizing a study tour on institutions and policy instruments

The second project, "Integrated forestry management in Albania" aims at complex policy and institutional reform in the country through the reorganization of the Albanian General Directorate of Forest and Pasture, improving management of the State forest, maintaining forest roads, improving communal forest management, and the development of management plans for 27 communes. The project, implemented in cooperation with the World Bank and FAO, has a budget of $21.6 million. The preparation and implementation of this large project were supported or complemented by some other projects; FAO provided assistance in the field of forestry and wildlife legislation in the preparatory phase; Austria organized one study tour and provided technical assistance in four additional sub-projects in 1997-98; Italy contributed to the strengthening of the environmental management, monitoring and assessment capacities, establishing a new institutional structure within the Ministry, training its staff, and setting up an information system to monitor the status of Albanian forests, and the socio-economic and environmental impacts of the project.

In a special regional cooperation in 1997 and 1998 Turkey organized two regional workshops for the southern CIS countries and Albania.

Albania also participated in the multi-country Phare project "Sustainable forestry and forest biodiversity conservation in central and eastern Europe".

With regard to future plans, Albania expressed interest in cooperating with organizations like ICP Forests, ECE, World Bank, FAO, UNDP, UNEP, GEF, IUFRO, EBRD, in the following areas:
- Sharing experiences in institutional strengthening and policy development.
- Sharing experiences and training in sustainable development of forests and forest production sectors.
- Strengthening trans-boundary cooperation in the environment and forest protection against damages, especially fires.

Bulgaria

Currently available reports list 26 projects. Although more projects were reported from the early years, missing pieces of information make the analysis quite difficult and no information is available on the scope of financial resources involved.

Earlier projects were focused mainly on disseminating knowledge through education, workshops and joint research. Austria, France and Germany played an important role in this cooperation.

Larger projects were developed in the late 1990s in cooperation with the WWF and Germany. The Green Balkan project was prepared in 1999 aiming to restore and rehabilitate the Danube region.

Switzerland contributed to two projects: "Sustainable Management of the Forests in Bulgaria" between 1997 and 2001 and the "Biodiversity Conservation Programme ".

Germany is contributing to providing support during the restitution process and consultancy for the newly established private forestry.

In cooperation with UNDP/GEF an important project was developed with a total funding need of about 10 million Leva, of which the source of about 6 million Leva is already identified. This is a five-year plan (from 1999 to 2003) to implement biodiversity conservation projects according to the National Biodiversity Conservation Plan.

Both GEF and USAID contributed to the Bulgaria Global Environment Facility Biodiversity Project focused on improving biodiversity conservation, sustainable use of biodiversity areas and integrated development of protected areas.

Bulgaria also participated in the multi-country Phare project "Sustainable forestry and forest biodiversity conservation in central and eastern Europe".

Belarus

Although Belarus did not respond to the questionnaires, it was possible to compile a list of projects, implemented mostly between 1995 and 1997.

Germany contributed to the research on the use of wood for energy and to the education of forestry experts.

Denmark allocated a sum of DKK 2.3 million for supporting an integrated control programme of *Lymantria monacha* and *Dendrolimus pini* in two projects, one of them jointly implemented with Poland. In 1997 Denmark together with the United States Department of Energy participated in a project aimed at the use of wood and litter with radioactive contamination for generating energy through combustion.

Finland supported the development of the Forestry Strategic Plan as part of the Forestry Development Project, addressing issues such as the environment and conservation, low levels of wood harvesting and production, stimulation of employment and improvement of the trade balance. The project was also to assist the government in defining the framework for policy adjustments in the forestry sector and identifying future investments. Finland offered $1.5 million to support the project. Another project focused on exploring the potential for GIS applications, and a project proposed to educate foresters through training courses in Finland.

In the year 2000, the United Kingdom offered a training session in a special course, which ended with a 10-day study tour in the UK.

Croatia

Little information is available from Croatia. One project on the development of new production management in wood processing and furniture manufacturing, which was in its planning phase at the time of the previous survey, was completed. Austria reported two study tours; Germany assisted in one IPGRI meeting.

➤ The large project "Coastal forest reconstruction and protection" with a budget of $67.3 million (of which $42 million came from the World Bank) was focused on three main areas between 1997-2002:

➤ Reconstruction of coastal forests destroyed by war.

➤ Forest fire management.

➤ Support services including institutional development of the state forest enterprise Hrvatska Sume (HS).

Since the World Bank fund is not used up totally, the remaining resources will be spent on completing the works on a forest nursery and the initial phase of HS restructuring.

Czech Republic

The cooperation under Resolution H3 was very active in the Czech Republic; the country reported 34 projects and an additional 49 projects could be found through other countries' reports. Workshops, seminars and conferences played an important role in this cooperation, several of them were also of regional importance, and were not only hosted but also co-sponsored by the Czech Republic. Many of them were focused on forest health and forest policy related issues (11th ICP Forests Task Force meeting 1995, Forest ecosystem restoration 1995, Level II forest health monitoring 1996, Tree seed pathology 1996, Atmospheric Deposition and Forest Management 1996, Forest insect an disease survey 1997, Conference on Forest policy in Countries with Economies in Transition - "ready for the European Union?" 1997, Forest certification and countries in transition 1998, 3rd meeting of *Picea abies* EUFORGEN network 1998, Seminar on "Forestry Research on the Threshold of the 3rd Millennium" 1998).

Between 1994 and 1997 Austria organized a series of 14 study tours on various topics of sustainable forest management. Germany and Sweden also contributed to study tours; the United Kingdom to educational opportunities.

Research and capacity building projects were also focused on forest condition. GEF financed a project of $170,000 on the restoration of forest ecosystems in the period of 1993-97. It supported:

➤ Purchase of new izo-enzyme equipment and the necessary chemicals to identify native populations of tree and plant species;

➤ Professional development and training in utilizing this equipment and undertaking wider conservation biology activities (organized in the Czech Republic and abroad);

➤ Investment in pilot programmes on forest restoration and conservation. Several small pilot programmes were started, e.g., purchase of special equipment for controlling the nun-moth;

➤ Purchase of deep freezers for a laboratory of biotechnology and of a stereomicroscope with microphotography equipment.

Co-sponsored by the United States an assessment of ozone concentration and its phytotoxicity was conducted in 1996. In 1997 the IUFRO and the United States helped to study the same topic in the Carpathian forests (Poland also took part in the study).

Four major projects financed by the EU were reported: Phare supported the forest sector study in 1994-95; Interreg II co-sponsored a beech case study in the Czech Republic, Austria and Germany; the Czech Republic also participated in the multi-country Phare project, "Sustainable forestry and forest biodiversity conservation in central and eastern Europe" and in the Inco-Copernicus project, "Scenario analysis of sustainable wood production under different forest management regimes (SCEFORMA)".

From 1998 to 2000, Phare Cross Border Cooperation sponsored a number of projects aimed at the rehabilitation of forest areas with heavy pollution damage. Two of these, Luzicke/Krusne and Hory mountains, (together with Germany) were completed in 2000. Another Phare project focused on "EU Training and Negotiations Preparation Training of State Officials in EU Affairs".

The cooperation with Germany resulted in a number of research projects focused mainly on forest vitality problems.

A new project on the strengthening of private and community forestry in central and eastern Europe is in preparation in cooperation with FAO.

Estonia

A strong "Nordic dimension" characterized the cooperation with Estonia - only 12 of the 52 reported projects were implemented with non-Nordic partners. It is also important to note that cooperation remained very intensive in the recent years (15 projects are from the period 1998 onwards).

Contrary to the previous inventory when only one project was reported, information on several large projects was provided. With Danish help of DKK 9.5 million, a forest conservation area network was created between 1999-2001. Sweden is contributing to the full-scale Woodland Key Habitat Inventory in Estonia with a budget of EEK 9.4 million. Finland and Sweden jointly work with Estonia in a LIFE-funded project on the reconstruction of wooded meadows and pastures in Saaremaa.

In the field of SFM, Finland assisted in the establishment of demonstration areas to illustrate ways and means of forest management practices and planning. Sweden provided EEK 880,000 for a project on the sustainable management of deciduous forests. The Phare programme supported the establishment of the Foundation of Private Forest Centre with EEK 4.7 million in the period 1998-2000.

Estonia hosted a number of important events, such as the Meeting of Forestry Societies of Baltic States (Sagadi, Estonia, 15-16 August 2001), and The Baltic 21 Forest Sector Meeting, (Sagadi, Estonia, 26-28.09.2001). One of the series of the FAO/ECE workshops on development of marketing of sawnwood products was also organised in Estonia.

In addition to the above projects reported by Estonia, the donor countries also reported intense cooperation. Six projects from Germany cover a wide range of activities from training to research and support to forestry administration. Among others, Denmark contributed to the development of Sustainable Management Strategy for Estonian Forested Wetlands in the period 1997-98 with DKK 2.1 million. Finland reported eleven more projects with a focus on education, know-how transfer and capacity building (mostly between 1992-1996). The United Kingdom contributed to the Baltic States Rural Development Project with GBP 1.8 million in the three Baltic States between 2000-2003. Sweden participated in eight projects, aimed at education and training.

Hungary

The reported number of projects has increased considerably since the last survey. Development of human resources played an important role in the cooperation. Based on bilateral agreements with Germany (especially Baden-Württemberg) and Austria on expert exchange, a series of study tours were completed on a wide range of subjects, and Hungary also hosted experts from these countries. To facilitate intra-regional cooperation similar arrangements were set up on ministerial or institutional level with Russia, Poland and Slovakia.

Together with the Czech Republic and Slovakia as well as Austria and Germany as donor countries, Hungary participated in the project on differential diagnosis of oak damage in the Danube region in 1992-94.

The research cooperation with Austria resulted in two projects in 2000. The United Kingdom provided a PhD course and internship for forestry experts.

Hungary participated in a number of multilateral projects, such as the Inco-Copernicus programme, "Scenario analysis of sustainable wood production under different forest management regimes (SCEFORMA)" in 1998-2001; the INTERREG II.C No. 97005/ "Natural Resources" in 1999-2000; the "Scientific background of reforestation and afforestation improvement activities in Carpathian mountains" in 2000; and the multi-country Phare programme (for details see Slovakia).

The EU through the Phare programme contributed substantially to the development of the forest sector in Hungry. A sector screening was financed in 1993, followed by the State and private sectors, which were screened and analyzed separately in two projects. The potential uses of wood were analyzed in 2001. French, Irish (twice) and Swedish experts were contracted within these Phare projects. Quite recently the institutional development project of the forestry administration was implemented in a twinning programme with Germany and Austria between 2002-2003. This is the first project, which also has a supply component, resulting in a modernized communication and IT environment.

FAO contributed to a regional development project from its TCP in the Bujak region, and to a capacity building project in the private forestry sector for several countries of the region (including Hungary), financed also from TCP.

Hungary contributed to international cooperation by hosting various events, like the 13th Task Force meeting of ICP Forests; the UNECE workshop on marketing of wood and wood products; and recently in cooperation with the MCPFE Liaison Unit, the 3rd workshop on improving the pan-European C&I for SFM.

Latvia

Latvia has not reported new projects since the last survey. However, there was a great deal of cooperative projects in the second half of the 1990s (especially with Germany). Compared to the two projects reported in 1996, the current dataset has information on twenty four projects. This is mostly due to the cooperation between the Ministry for Environment of North Rhine-Westphalia and the University of Jeglava, which resulted in twenty-three education and training projects.

Contributions from Denmark were also substantial. In thirteen projects Denmark allocated DKK 31 million for assistance. These projects covered a wide range of issues including education and training for: sawmilling, private forestry, key forestry administrators, inventory of species and habitats, protection of sensitive species, land consolidation and management plans for protection areas.

Besides the Baltic States Rural Development Project, the United Kingdom contributed to a number of projects aimed at private forestry development, certification, ecological planning and institutional development.

Latvia also participated in the multi-country Phare project (for details see Slovakia).

Lithuania

The second half of the 1990s brought intensive cooperation. While there were only thirty projects reported in the second survey in 1996, the latest dataset contains eighty-six projects of which forty-five were reported by Lithuania. The cooperation is characterised by a Nordic dominance, most of the projects were implemented with Danish, Finnish and Swedish help, but Germany also contributed considerably. Most of the projects were focused on education/training and research (28 and 21 respectively).

The cooperation with Sweden is an important element; twenty-five projects of different size were reported. Between 1993-1998 a Forest Sector Development Plan was developed with a budget of SEK 5.4 million. In 1996 Sweden helped the Lithuanian forest sector development programme with a project on national monitoring and management information, followed by national forest inventory and dynamic modelling. In 2000, SEK 1.4 million was allocated for developing the utilisation of wood for fuel. The second phase of the project continued in 2001-2002.

The Dubrava Experimental Forest Enterprise enjoyed considerable support in four different projects, of which two were supported by the Phare programme and two by Denmark. The EU also contributed to training tree-nursery and sawmilling workers, and Lithuania participated in the multi-country Phare programme.

Among nineteen different projects, Denmark supported the State Park Institutional Development Project in 1997-2000 with DKK 9.5 million. Denmark also supported "Afforestation of abandoned agricultural land based on sustainable planning and environmentally sound forest management" in 1999-2001 with LTL 3.9 million, and supported a project on developing sustainable private forestry in 1996 and 1997.

Nine projects implemented with Finnish help were focused on different issues including: statistical and information systems, education and sawmilling. An important project on "Forest development strategy and implementation under the market economy conditions in Birzai Forest Enterprise" aimed at forestry operations according to the market analysis and production possibilities with the goal to improve information usage, environmentally sound technology, sustainable utilisation of natural resources, effective marketing and sales, improved capabilities of the staff and increased economical efficiency.

Germany supported twelve projects of a smaller dimension, focusing mostly on education and research.

Together with the other two Baltic States, Lithuania participates in the "Baltic States Rural Development Project" sponsored by the UK. This multifaceted project supports human resource development across a range of industries including forestry and wood processing.

FAO contributed $67,000 to the control of nun moth in 1995, and $247,000 to a project on developing the private forestry sector in 1998-2000.

Poland

The number of projects implemented in Poland increased considerably from the previous reporting period. Austria organised study tours on several aspects of forestry between 1994-1997 (none of them included in the previous report).

Germany has assisted in 15 projects so far, most of them aimed at dissemination of knowledge through study tours and workshops. Research projects were targeted on a wide range of subjects, from dendrochronology to production and marketing of particle boards and analysis of wood products markets.

The cooperation with Denmark was characterised by know-how transfer and financial assistance in eleven projects. These included: the control of nun moth, utilization of wood chips and residues, introduction of multiple use concept to SFM and afforestation of marginal agricultural land. The total amount involved in these projects was at least DKK 24 million.

Six projects were completed in cooperation with the UK, of which the largest was the Phare-financed Forestry Development Programme between 1994-1997.

An interesting agreement was set up between Italy and Poland on the conversion of the debts of $32.6 million into Environmental Protection initiatives (Ekofundus) in the period 1998-2009.

Since 1996 Poland reported only three new projects: "Development of selected forestry branches and protection of ecosystems in National Parks in 1993-1997", "Forest biodiversity protection project", "Use of GIS and Satellite Remote Sensing for monitoring afforestation at regional and local levels". These projects were successfully completed. The country also participated in the multi-country Phare project (for detail see Slovakia).

Poland participated in a number of intra-regional projects, such as the "Evaluation of ozone air pollution and its phytotoxic potential in the Carpathian forests" with the Czech Republic. Four countries from the region participated in intra-regional projects financed by the United States on the "Effects of Air Pollution on Forests Health and Biodiversity in forests of the Carpathian Mountains (Programme of IUFRO-SPDC)". The Inco-Copernicus programme "SCEFORMA" and the multi-country Phare projects are also excellent examples of regional cooperation.

Romania

There was only one project reported from Romania: "Genetic resources of broad-leaved forest tree species in southern Europe", (coordinated by IPGRI, Rome), in which Romania participates together with other countries. The first phase took place in 1997-2000 and the second phase is scheduled for 2001-2003.

In 1994 Austria provided phytopathology training. With a budget of €500,000, Germany completed a project on promotion of education in the field of environmental protection (TEMPUS); Germany also contributed to dendrochronology research and to expanding forestry education on environmental protection.

Denmark allocated DKK 4.7 million for sustainable management and biological conservation of the Ceahlau Nature Reserve in 1997.

France contributed to the development of research. The United Kingdom supported certification programmes and some activities of environmental NGOs.

Romania also participated in the multi-country Phare programme, and regional cooperation such as an investigation of air pollution effects, and the afforestation of the Carpathian region.

Russian Federation

Compared to the forty-six reports in the previous survey, the current dataset contains 105 projects of which twelve were reported by the Russian Federation.

Austria contributed to two research projects in 1995-97 on developing a simulation model for forests affected by human activities and a study on the spruce grouse.

Switzerland allocated CHF 2 million for the Pechoro-Ilych Model Project in 1995-1999. The project resulted in securing the Pechoro-Ilych Reserve, development of models for sustainable boreal forests and training and education.

Germany cooperated in twenty-four projects. One of the largest of these projects (with a budget of DEM 415,000) started in 1991 and focused on long-term forest ecosystem monitoring of climatologic conditions, deposition of atmospheric pollutants, water and element budgets, water quality and forest health and yield. A forest ecosystem monitoring network was also established, and a complete monitoring station (similar to those used in "Bayerische Waldklimastationen") was installed in the "Central Forest Biosphere Reservation". Between 1996-2000, five seminars/workshops were conducted on forest economics.

Denmark contributed to the development of:
➢ ecotourism and nature protection in the Kaliningrad Region with DKK 1.3 million;
➢ Centre for Nature and Environment, St. Petersburg (Pushkin) with DKK 3.2 million;
➢ the Kaliningrad Eco-Centre, with DKK 2 million:
➢ the Valdai National Park;
➢ sustainable management of Sebezsky National Park with DKK 1.4 million;
➢ integrating protected areas in a regional context with DKK 6.9 million ; and
➢ the project "Understanding of Environment and of Nature in Kaliningrad" with DKK 1.5 million.

Twenty nine projects were implemented in cooperation with Finland. All of them were included in the previous survey as ongoing or planned projects. With the exception of a long term thinning research project, all of them were completed successfully (although no information is available on the planned Lake Ladoga Symposium). The known amount involved in the completed projects was $2.2 million; the ongoing project on thinning has a budget of FIM 700,000.

In 1997 the United Kingdom in cooperation with the World Bank contributed to examining the current state-of-the-art forest information systems with regard to their efficient capture, storage, analysis and retrieval of forest resources information for use in forest management planning and control. Between 1994-1997 the United Kingdom Forestry Commission and the United States Forest Service conducted study tours. The United Kingdom recently supported Russian participation in the Kyoto Conference, and assisted in the development of a policy framework for national parks with a budget of £920,000.

Norway financed seventeen projects, mostly focusing on education and training, but considerable attention was also paid to the joint activities in logging and sawmilling. For example the Telemark Wood Company invested NOK 35 million in a joint venture in Vologda.

Russia reported twelve projects of which eleven were sponsored by NIPIEIlesprom. In 1997-1999 a programme on restructuring the forest and forest products sector was implemented in the Komi, Bashkortostan and Udmurt Republics and in the Kovrov and Vologda Regions. Additionally, in 1999 large-scale studies were carried out, such as an analysis of: the status of integration processes in the forest and forest products sector, and systems for managing production costs at forest and forest products enterprises. This programme obviously plays an important role in the development of the forest sector in Russia, but its link to Resolution H3 is not clear.

A massive project of $60 million is being implemented with financial assistance from the EBRD. The prime target of the project is to provide support to key areas of forest sector reforms and forest policy development including, *inter alia*:

➢ strengthening public sector administration and governance, which are essential for the forest sector management;

➢ establishing an enabling environment for private sector development;

➢ strengthening the institutional framework necessary for the enforcement of existing laws and regulations on the environment, natural resources and forest management.

The desired goals in these key areas will be achieved by implementing activities in two main project components:

➢ Component A: Support to the sustainable management of the public forests

➢ Component B: Support to improving the regional forest enterprise management

In order to achieve measurable results over a period of three to five years, it was decided to limit initially the interventions to three pilot regions - Leningrad Oblast in European Russia, Krasnoyarsk Kray in Central Siberia, and Khabarovsk Kray in the Far East.

The cooperation with Sweden resulted in a number of projects aimed at disseminating information and knowledge, capacity building in forest cadastre, utilisation of wood for fuel and model forests.

Slovakia

With nineteen projects of which nine are new in the dataset, Germany proved to be the key partner in H3-related cooperation with Slovakia. Most of these projects aimed at research, such as: "Technology for products from black locust" in 1996 with an amount of €215,000, or the "Differential diagnosis of oak damage in the Danube region" (together with the Czech Republic and Hungary) in 1994-1996 with DEM 600,000. The COST Action E2 wood durability (in cooperation with Slovenia and Germany) enjoyed a support of DEM 60,000 annually between 1994-1998.

Slovakia played a key role in preparing the multi-country Phare project proposal on "Sustainable forestry and forest biodiversity conservation in central and eastern Europe", and when the proposal was accepted, Slovakia became the coordinator of this project with a budget of €600,000. The first phase of this originally two-phased project aimed at a detailed analysis of the forest sector in thirteen CITs. Based on this analysis, the second phase would have included investments needed for the implementation of SFM. Unfortunately, the second phase has not been implemented. Nevertheless, the analysis seems to be the most comprehensive and up-to-date study of the CITs forest sector so far.

Education and training was supported by a number of projects from the United Kingdom and Sweden.

Slovenia

Slovenia reported few new projects since the last survey. Two new research projects were: the first on brown bears in Slovenia/Karinthia (with a budget of $128,000), and the second, on the ecology of the lynx and bear populations in Slovenia with a budget of $152,000. Austria contributed to the implementation of one institution-building project supporting the foundation of a private forestry association in Slovenia.

Together with Slovakia and Germany, Slovenia participated in the Cost action E2 on wood durability. Slovenia also participated in the multi-country Phare programme.

Ukraine

A number of new projects were reported on cooperation with Ukraine. In 1993 Ukraine together with the Czech Republic, participated in a project on restoration of forest ecosystems — a Global Environment Facility/Biodiversity Protection Project.

Germany cooperated with Ukraine on the Tempus-TACIS preparatory project on setting up new study courses on natural resource economics at the Ukrainian State University of Forestry and Wood Technology.

From 1997 to 1999 the United Kingdom assisted Ukraine in sustainable tourism development in protected areas. In 1998-1999, the United Kingdom assisted Ukrainian NGOs to use the UN system effectively to promote environmental activities.

In 1998 Liechtenstein contributed to a project on private agro-forestry development and provided practical training for sustainable use of alpine forests in 2000.

From 1998 to 2000 Sweden organised study tours and contributed to the preparation of the Forest Sector Master Plan.

Ukraine reported the following new projects:

➤ The project on legal, administrative and policy strategies for securing sustainable development of the forest sector in Russia, Belarus and Ukraine (INTAS programme), 1996-1998;

➤ The project on the Effects of Air Pollution on Forests Health and Biodiversity in Forests of the Carpathian Mountains (Programme of IUFRO-SPDC) (supported by the United States and implemented in 1997-2001, together with four other CITs. The project on forest certification of 4 forestry enterprises under the FSC scheme;

➤ The project on "Nature values in the East and West: biodiversity - native forests - protection territories", (these last two projects were supported by Switzerland in 2000-2001);

➤ The project on "Scenario analysis of sustainable wood production under different forest management regimes (SCEFORMA) (INCO-Copernicus programme)";

➤ The intra-regional cooperation project on the "Scientific background of reforestation and afforestation improvement activities in the Carpathian mountains".

Figure 6

Number of projects reported by transition countries not signatories to H3

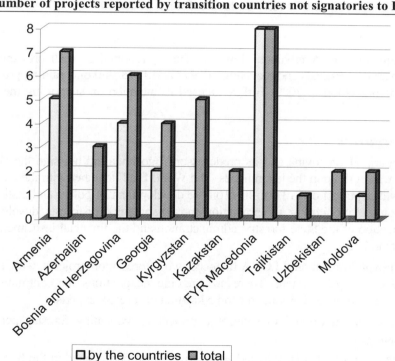

Source: H3 database

6.2.2 NON-SIGNATORY COUNTRIES IN TRANSITION

Armenia

In the period 1994-97, FAO conducted one large project in Armenia within the Technical Cooperation Programme. The project had a budget of $380,000 and included:

➢ training;
➢ trial wood sale auctions;
➢ a national forestry workshop;
➢ the preparation of a new forest policy and strategy, and review of forest regulations;
➢ the preparation of an associated portfolio of investment profiles;
➢ the preparation of the Institutional Capacity Building (ICB) Project on behalf of UNDP.

In 1998 and 1999, the World Bank sponsored the preparation of an Armenian National Environmental Action Plan focusing on the development of an institutional and regulatory framework for environmental management. The budget of the project was $200,000.

In the same years, Sweden helped in arranging and carrying out the Forest Resource Assessment (FRA) of the Armenian forests suitable for utilization. The project aimed to get strategic data necessary for the decisions in forest management policies. SIDA allocated for the project SEK 1.8 million.

In 2000, with the aim of supporting SFM, the United Kingdom sponsored the development of forest certification standards. The total cost of the project was £20,000.

The World Bank Joint Environmental Programme (JEP-06) and the EU TACIS programme have contributed with a budget of $200,000 to the preparation of the forest management component of the " Natural Resources Management and Poverty Reduction Project - Armenia".

Azerbaijan

No report is available from Azerbaijan. However, Turkey reported 3 small projects: two meetings on regional cooperation and on residues and recycling in 1997 and 1998, and one training programme on erosion control and arid zone plantation in 2000. Turkey focused its attention on supporting the Central-Asian CIS countries.

Bosnia and Herzegovina

Although Bosnia and Herzegovina and its predecessor Yugoslavia did not sign the Helsinki resolutions, intensive assistance was built up in the late nineties. The World Bank together with the EU, Italy and Norway financed a project with a budget of $13.4 million on the development of policy and institutional framework, management planning and monitoring, the protection and rehabilitation of forests, development of the wood processing, reorganization of the State forestry, administration and the financial instruments. The project was expected to terminate in 2001.

Two NGOs -, Nuovua Frontera and LORA financed two afforestation projects, which were implemented quite independently of the government. There are ongoing negotiations for continuing the project with Nuovua Frontera in the field of seed production and education of forestry experts.

The government of Japan offered to sponsor a project on educating forestry personnel to promote sustainable forest management.

Together with the other 13 CITs Bosnia and Herzegovina also participated in the first phase of the multi-country Phare project on "Sustainable forestry and forest biodiversity conservation in Central and Eastern Europe".

Georgia

Although no report is available from Georgia, some projects were retrieved from the dataset. In 1997 Austria, with financial assistance from the World Bank, organized a study tour for the Georgian Forestry Department to study the institutional framework and its functioning. In 1999 and 2000 the United Kingdom (namely the Edinburgh City Council) sponsored a local study to assess the growth potential of plants for medical and homeopathic purposes and to recommend improvements to the sheep farming industry.

In 1997 the World Bank Institutional Development Fund assisted in developing the Georgian National Forestry Strategy. On this basis and with further assistance from the World Bank and FAO, a forestry development programme was prepared to restructure the organization and functioning of the forest sector.

Kyrgyzstan

Very limited information is available on the cooperation projects in Kyrgyzstan. From 1995 to 1997 Switzerland participated in a project on developing the forest sector towards environmental and economic sustainability. Switzerland allocated CHF 2 million for the project. Turkey sponsored three regional meetings (for details see Azerbaijan).

Kazakhstan

With the exception of two regional meetings organized by Turkey (for details see Azerbaijan), no information is available on the cooperation with Kazakhstan.

The FYR of Macedonia

Most of the projects reported were in the planning phase. Two projects were completed:
➤ a multi country Phare project (for details see Slovakia);
➤ a project on biological control of *Thaumatopoea pityocampa Schiff* that was carried out in cooperation with Italy and France in 1997-2000 (with a budget of DEM 51,000).

The planned research projects are focused on air pollution, selection of seed plantations, productivity of beech, and vegetative compatibility of *Cryphonectria parasitica*.

Republic of Moldova

In 1998 Finland assisted in drawing up strategies and working out the implementation and action plans for sustainable development of the forest sector in Moldova and allocated $100,000 for this purpose.

"PRIRODA" is a cooperative environment technology programme established in 1992 between the authorities, research institutions and companies in Norway (and originally also in north-western Russia) to focus on environmental problems. The programme was expanded in 1995 to include several joint venture projects.

Tajikistan

Only Turkey reported one regional meeting where Tajikistan participated.

Turkmenistan

With the exception of two regional meetings organized by Turkey (for details see Azerbaijan), no information is available on the cooperation with Turkmenistan.

Uzbekistan

With the exception of two regional meetings organized by Turkey (for details see Azerbaijan), no information is available on the cooperation with Uzbekistan.

Figure 7
Reported number of projects by countries in the H3 database

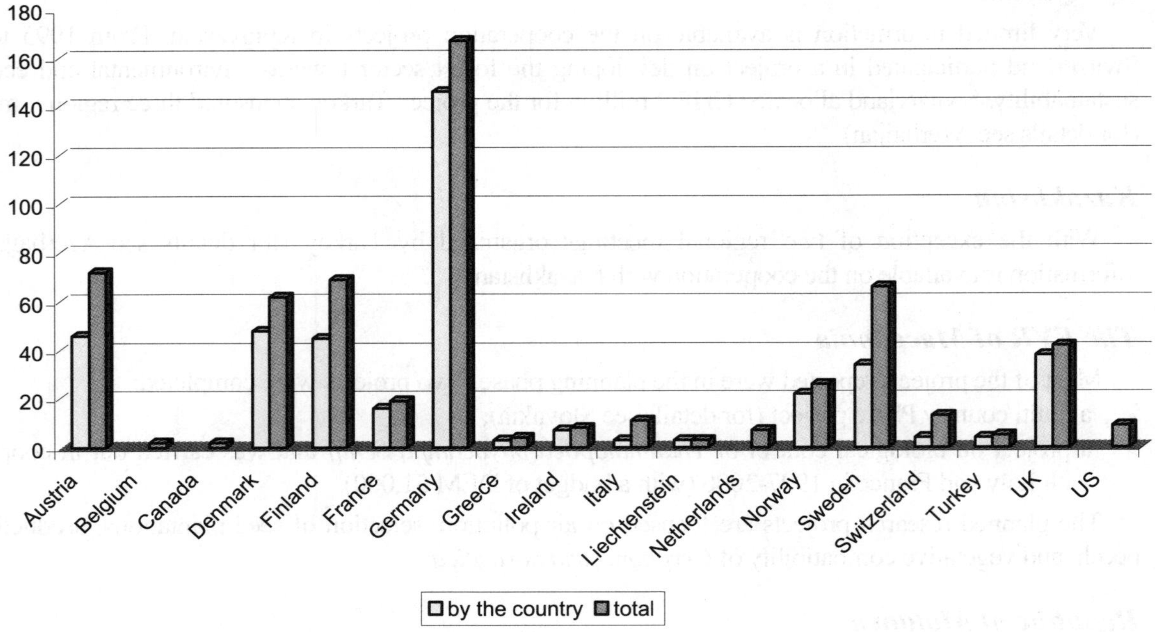

Source: H3 database

6.3   *Activities of the donor countries/organizations*

Countries of the donor community reported a total of 419 projects. However more projects were identified from the reports of the transition countries (please note that multiple reporting is not excluded from the series "total").

The majority of the projects were reported by seven countries: Germany, Denmark, Austria, Finland, Sweden, United Kingdom and Norway.

Germany took part in several projects on the federal level, but also through her *Laender*. About 40% of the reported projects focused on research; 35% on study tours, workshops and seminars; and 24% on education and training. The projects are fairly evenly distributed over the last decade with a slight decrease at the end of the 1990s. Most of the cooperation was aimed at the Czech Republic, Hungary, Latvia, Lithuania, Poland, Russia and Slovakia.

Almost two third of the Austrian projects were study tours, seminars and workshops. Research, technical assistance and capacity building constitute about 15% of the reported projects. Most of the projects were implemented in the period 1995-1997. The neighbour countries of Austria benefited the most from this cooperation.

Cooperation with the Scandinavian countries targeted mostly the CITs of Northern Europe, notably the Baltic States and Russia. Beside the work within the UN and MCPFE, this cooperation is mostly based on regional agreements and programmes, such as the Baltic 21 and the Barents Euro-Arctic Council networks. The latter, through its forest sector programme, aims at policy development, investments to improve conditions for SFM, participation and education, and development of forestry operations. The forestry element of the Baltic 21 network focuses on promotion of wood use, information and experiences exchange, establishment of demonstration areas for implementing SFM, and gap analysis of forest conservation in the region.

International organisations reported 24 projects, but obviously they were involved in many more. This indicates that there is a potential for improving coordination with such organisations.

Due to the improvement of the quality of the dataset, it became known that the three main pillars of the cooperation with the CITs in the forestry area are the EU, FAO and the World Bank. The number of projects financed by the EU and the World Bank increased considerably and was particularly noteworthy. The evolution of EU projects correlates very strongly with the evolution of the Phare and TACIS programmes. The World Bank sponsored a wide range of projects, from strategy development to rehabilitation of degraded forest areas.

Figure 8

Reported number of projects by organizations in the H3 database

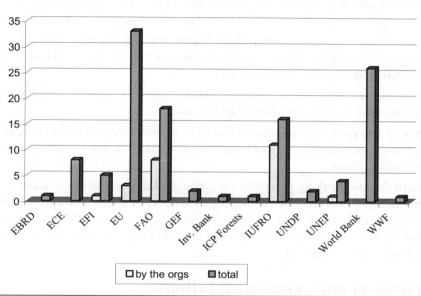

Source: H3 database

Although the UNECE has a limited budget and human resources, it made considerable contributions to transferring knowledge by organizing workshops and seminars. The UNECE also promoted the cross-regional cooperation in Europe by stimulating the preparation of country profiles and carrying out special studies such as the European Forest Sector Outlook Studies (EFSOS) and the Forest Resources Assessments (FRA).

The role of the European Forest Institute (EFI) has increased since the second round of monitoring, and the institute has contributed to a number of research projects in the CIT region.

IUFRO provided travel grants for scientists from CITs in the first half of the nineties. More recently it contributed to organizing workshops and seminars on different subjects.

6.4   Emerging and evolving issues in the CITs during the last decade

At the beginning of the transition period, most of the focus was on the direct effects and side-effects of the transition, such as restitution and disturbances arising from the shrinking economy. At the time of the second survey (1995), a clear diversification of issues was noted. The emerging issues were SFM, need for investment and raising awareness. Cross-sectoral issues were not often the focus of attention.

The most recent reports from the countries suggest that different aspects of SFM are still of a very high importance (especially environmental protection and socio-economic dimensions). Many countries recognize the need for developing integrated forest, land use, and conservation policies, as well as a sound information base (including criteria and indicators for SFM) and efficient means of its management. Many countries see national forest programmes as important tools for implementation of SFM, and not only as an obligation arising from the voluntary commitments arising from the following international forestry dialogue.

Accordingly, an increasing number of countries recognize the role of public awareness and the multi-stakeholder dialogue in developing forest policies, and see this as an important topic for international cooperation. Policies and programmes should be based on sound factual and scientific bases, but also on a wide consensus within the society, which can hardly be reached without successfully communicating forestry issues.

Restitution and privatization are still important issues in the CIT countries, which are well into the privatization process, especially regarding the economic feasibility of SFM implementation in small private holdings. Countries, which have started the restitution and privatization process recently, or are planning to do so, may face the same type of problems as more advanced countries experienced at the same phase of their development. There is an enormous potential for intra-regional cooperation in this field.

Institutional and capacity building is still of high importance, but it is especially critical in those countries where foreseen accession to the European Union has brought a new dimension to this work, and whose needs arise from implementing the *acquis communautaire*.

Afforestation is an important issue in several countries; partly because it is related to the accession, but also because of its scientific, technical and financial dimensions.

There are special needs recognized among the CITs as well. Due to unfortunate developments in the Balkan region, environmental protection and forestry development largely concern post-war rehabilitation of degraded areas including forests.

The report from the two working groups of the Dębe workshop contains the most comprehensive list of needs and priority areas of concern (see chapter 5.4). However, it should be born in mind that some of the CITs, especially those in Central Asia, are lacking links and communication channels to the ongoing cooperation under MCPFE, UNECE/FAO or other instruments/organizations. Therefore, very little is known at present about their needs and problems.

7   Conclusions and recommendations

The countries with economies in transition have gone through a considerable evolution since the last survey in 1995. The region has become more diverse and the problems cover a much wider range of issues than at the beginning of the transition period. On the other hand, there is a quite rich pool of experience available, whereas at the beginning of the transition one of the major concerns was that it was an unprecedented process with no patterns readily available in the market economies.

Several countries have established a significant private forestry sector, while others have been more cautious in introducing such changes. These different approaches could be observed also on the macro-economic scale. It seems (for the time being) that countries taking the "faster track" were able to produce higher economic growth in recent years than those who have moved more slowly. This also contributed to the diversification of the region.

In spite of these divergences, there is a core set of issues, which has been the focus of attention for many years: economically viable, multifunctional, sustainable forest management, and its enabling legal and financial environment, the conservation and extension of forest resources, the development of the institutional framework for public and private forestry as well as for forestry administration, the increasing of public awareness and involvement in forestry matters, and recognition of the cross-sectoral nature of most forestry issues.

The special problems and conditions of the transition countries were recognized by many political fora giving further and continued internal and external support to the cooperation within and outside the H3 context. This political support resulted in extensive implementation of the H3 commitments.

Most of the reported projects aimed at the dissemination of information, knowledge and experiences; roughly 50% were study tours, workshops and training programmes; joint research activities represented roughly 20%; among other types of cooperation, the development of policies and strategies represented a considerable share.

It is important to note that relevant information may be missing from major donor countries and financing organizations. The experiences with the existing dataset show that the missing information cannot be fully recovered from the reports of the beneficiary countries. There is an acute lack of reports from Canada, the United States, the World Bank and the EBRD and possibly significant under reporting. This limits the comprehensiveness of analyses based on the information available.

The cooperation between UNECE/FAO and MCPFE has resulted in a better understanding of problems and a clearer definition of the needs of the CITs, which were involved in these activities. For those countries, which were not involved in these cooperative projects (many countries of the former USSR), the identification of problems remained difficult. It is very likely that the countries, which are most in need, will miss the benefits from this international cooperation. It is advisable that UNECE should seek ways to establish information channels to these countries.

When setting priorities for future cooperation and assistance to the CITs, the outcome of the recent work should be considered. Besides the cooperation with the donor community, it would be extremely important to make the best use of the experiences gathered so far by increasing intra-regional cooperation. This would require increasing the transparency of the process.

With relatively little additional work the usefulness of the H3 database could be increased and a high added value could be gained. The information in the H3 database should be improved through increased communication with the countries involved, elimination of known discrepancies and filling-in the missing pieces of information. Countries and organizations which have not provided information so far should be encouraged to provide the information needed in the H3 database. The Timber Committee together with the European Forestry Commission as well as the Expert Level Follow-up Meeting of MCPFE may wish to consider proposals aimed at achieving this.

References:

CSD: REVIEW OF SECTORAL CLUSTERS. Report of the *Ad Hoc* Intergovernmental Panel on Forests on its second session. E/CN.17/1996/24. New York, 1996

CSD: Report of the Intergovernmental Forum on Forests on its third session. E/CN.17/2000/14. New York 2000

CSD: Report of the *Ad Hoc* Intergovernmental Panel on Forests on its third session. E/CN.17/IPF/1997/2 New York, 1997

CSD: Report of the *Ad Hoc* Intergovernmental Panel on Forests on its fourth session. E/CN.17/1997/12. New York, 1997

Csóka, P.: Interim Report on the Implementation of Resolution H3 of the Helsinki Ministerial Conference on the Protection of Forests in Europe. Results of the second enquiry. ECE/TIM/DP/12. United Nations, New York and Geneva, 1997

Csóka, P.: The Role of the Private Sector, Economies in Transition and Issues of Privatisation in Forestry. Special paper prepared for the XI World Forestry Congress. In Proceedings of the XI World Forestry Congress, FAO, 1997

Csóka, P.: Forest Policy Activities in the Countries in Transition in their Preparation for the EU. In Forest Policy in the Countries with Economies in Transition - Ready for the European Union? EFI Proceedings No.21, 1998, European Forest Institute, 1998

Csóka, P.: The forests in countries in transition – a case study. In Report of the IUFRO Task Force on Environmental Change: The socio-economic implications of environmental change with particular relevance to forestry. (To be published in 2002)

ECOSOC: Report of the Ad Hoc Intergovernmental Panel on Forests on its first session. E/CN.17/IPF/1995/3. New York, 1995

ECOSOC: REPORT OF THE INTERGOVERNMENTAL FORUM ON FORESTS ON ITS FIRST SESSION. E/CN.17/IFF/1997/4. New York 1997

ECOSOC: Report of the Intergovernmental Forum on Forests on its second session. E/CN.17/IFF/1998/14. New York 1998

FAO: REPORT of the TWELFTH SESSION of the COMMITTEE ON FORESTRY COFO-1995/REP

FAO: REPORT of the THIRTEENTH SESSION of the COMMITTEE ON FORESTRY COFO-1997/REP

FAO: REPORT of the FOURTEENTH SESSION of the COMMITTEE ON FORESTRY COFO-1999/REP

FAO: THE FAO STRATEGIC PLAN FOR FORESTRY. Rome 1999

FAO Council: REPORT OF THE FIFTEENTH SESSION OF THE COMMITTEE ON FORESTRY CL 120/8, Rome 2001

Liaison Unit: Forests and Forestry in Central and Eastern European Countries. The Transition Process and Challenges Ahead. Vienna, 2002

Liaison Unit: Work Programme on the Follow-up of the Ministerial Conferences on the Protection of Forests in Europe. Vienna, 2000

Prins, C.: Forestry Co-operation with Countries with Economies in Transition – Resolution H3. In Follow-up Reports on the Ministerial Conferences on the Protection of Forests in Europe, Volume I. Lisbon, 1998

UNCED: Agenda 21 Chapter 11 -Combating Deforestation. Rio de Janeiro, 1992

UNCED: Agenda 21 Non-Legally Binding Authoritative Statement of Principles for a Global Consensus on the Management, Conservation and Sustainable Development of all Types of Forests. Rio de Janeiro, 1992

UNECE: Interim Report on the Implementation of Resolution H3 of the Helsinki Ministerial Conference on the Protection of Forests in Europe. Results of the first enquiry. Working paper. Geneva, 1994

UNECE/FAO: Forest Resources of Europe, CIS, North America, Australia, Japan and New Zealand (Industrialized temperate/boreal countries) UN-ECE/FAO contribution to the Global Forest Resources Assessment 2000. Main Report. ECE/TIM/SP/17. United Nations, New York and Geneva, 2000

UNECE/FAO: International Workshop "Forests and Forestry in Central and Eastern European Countries – the Transition Process and Challenges Ahead". Minutes of the Meeting. Geneva, 2001

UNECE Timber Committee: Report of the Committee on its Fifty-Ninth Session. ECE/TIM/97. Geneva 2001

UNECE Timber Committee/FAO European Forestry Commission: Report of the Joint Session. ECE/TIM/95. Geneva/Rome 2000

Annex I

List of projects by countries in transition as of June 2002

H3 Projects, Recipient Country: *Albania*

Project ID		Organization	Position	Cooperation	Title	Status	From/in	To	Type 1	Type 2	Type 3
AL001	AL	Albania	Recipient	Bilateral	Private forestry/Agroforestry development	Completed	1995	1998	Education/training	Capacity building	Know-how transfer
	AL	USAID	Donor			Completed	1995	1998	Education/training	Capacity building	Know-how transfer
AL002	AL	World Bank	Donor	Multilateral	Integrated forestry management in Albania	Ongoing	0	0	Education/training	Technical development	Capacity building
	US	FAO	Donor			Ongoing	0	0	Education/training	Technical development	Capacity building
	AL	General Directorate of Forests and Pastures (GDFP)	Recipient			Ongoing	0	0	Education/training	Technical development	Capacity building
AL003	AL	GEF	Donor	Multilateral	Projects under planning in cooperation with ICP Forest, ECE, World Bank, FAO, UNDP, UNEP, GEF, IUFRO, EBRD on the areas mentioned under the "contents"	In planning	0	0			
	FA	ICP Forest	Donor								
	WB	UNDP	Donor								
	AL	UNEP	Donor								
	DP	World Bank	Donor								
	EC	IUFRO	Donor								
	EP	GDFP	Recipient								
	FA	UNECE	Donor								
	FO	FAO	Donor								
AT012	GF	GDFP	Recipient	Trilateral	Study Tour--Forest Policy in Austria	Completed	1997	0	Study tour		
AT021	IP	GDFP	Recipient	Multilateral	Albanian forestry project: Review and improvement of Forest and Pasture Legislation	Completed	1997	0	Policy/strategy	Technical assistance	
AT022	WB	GDFP	Recipient	Multilateral	Albanian Forestry Project: Training of trainers of the Technical Forestry School of Shkodra	Completed	1997	0	Technical assistance		
AT023	AL	GDFP	Recipient	Multilateral	Albanian Forestry Project: Preparation of guidelines for Forest Management Plans	Completed	1997	0	Technical assistance		
AT024	AL	GDFP	Recipient	Multilateral	Albanian Forestry Project: Environmental mgmt. of forest roads and training of local experts for forest roads rehabilitation	Completed	1997	0	Technical assistance		
AT025	AL	GDFP	Recipient	Multilateral	Albanian Forestry Project: Definition of further steps for the preparation of management plan of NP Lura	Completed	1998	0	Technical assistance		
AT026	AL	GDFP	Recipient	Multilateral	Study Tour--Albanian experts at the Austrian Federal Forest Stock Company	Completed	1997	0	Study tour		
EU001	AL	Committee of Environmental Protection, Min. of Health and Envir. Protection	Recipient	Multilateral	Sustainable forestry and forest biodiversity conservation in central-eastern Europe	In planning	1997	1998	Scientific/research	Capacity building	Policy/strategy
FA001	AL		Recipient	Multilateral	Compendium of Computer-Based Databases of Relevance to Forest Products Marketing	Completed	1995	0	Capacity building		
FA006	AL	GDFP	Recipient	Multilateral	Integrated Forest Management Project (legal component)	completed	1992	1993	Policy/strategy		
FA007	AL	GDFP	Recipient	Multilateral	GCP/ALB/OUI/ITA	completed	1993	0	Policy/strategy		
FR012	AL	GDFP	Recipient	Multilateral	Strategy expertise for the preparation of an integrated forest project in Albania		1995	0	Policy/strategy		

H3 Projects, Recipient Country: *Albania (continued)*

Project ID		Organization	Position	Cooperation	Title	Status	From/in	To	Type 1	Type 2	Type 3
IT001	AL	MAF	Recipient	Trilateral	GCP/AIB/004/ITA, Technical assistance to the Forestry Project of Albania, funded by the World Bank	Ongoing	1996	2001	Education/training	Scientific/research	Technical development
TR001	AL		Recipient	Trilateral	Region cooperation meeting on forestry.	Completed	1997	0	Seminar/workshop		
TR002	AL		Recipient	Trilateral	Recycling, energy and market interactions	Completed	1998	0	Seminar/workshop		

H3 Projects, Recipient Country: *Bulgaria*

Project ID		Organization	Position	Cooperation	Title	Status	From/in	To	Type 1	Type 2	Type 3
AT001	BG	Committee of Forests	Recipient	Bilateral	Assessment and monitoring of air pollution effects on forests	Completed	1993	0	Education/training		
AT002	DP		Recipient	Bilateral	Study Tour--the Austrian Torrent and Avalanche System	Completed	1993	0	Study tour		
AT007	BG	Committee of Forests	Recipient	Bilateral	Forestry-related regional planning	Completed	1994	0	Seminar/workshop		
BG001	CH	Committee of Forests	Recipient	Bilateral	Forest Information System	In planning	1996	1997	Policy/strategy		
BG001	BG	Office National des Forets	Donor								
BG001	BG	Committee of Forests	Recipient								
BG002	BG	Committee of Forests	Recipient	Bilateral	United Forestry	Completed	1996	1996	Study tour		
BG002	BG	AFC/Ministry of Agriculture, Food and Forests	Donor								
BG003	BG	WWF	Donor	Multilateral	"Green-Balkan" Project (WWF/NF/NGO).	Completed	0	1999	Know-how transfer	Policy/strategy	Technical assistance
BG003	DE	Institute for Floodplain Ecology	Donor								
BG003	WW	Bulgaria	Recipient								
BG004	BG	Switzerland	Donor	Bilateral	Sustainable Management of the Forests in Bulgaria (Bulgarian-Swiss project - 1)	Ongoing	1997	2001	Technical assistance	"	"
BG004	BG	Bulgaria	Recipient	Bilateral							
BG005	FR	Bulgaria	Recipient	Bilateral	Restitution and Consultancy to Private Forest Owners (German-Bulgarian technical cooperation)	Ongoing	2001	0	Institutional development	"	"
BG005	BG	Germany	Donor	Bilateral							
BG006	BG	MoEW	Recipient	Multilateral	National Biodiversity Conservation Plan, Sofia 2000 (UNDP/GEF/MOEW)	Ongoing	1999	2003	Policy/strategy	"	"
BG006	DE	UNDP	Donor								
BG007	BG	GEF	Donor	Multilateral	Bulgaria Global Environment Facility Biodiversity Project (USAID(MOEW/GEF).		0	0	Institutional development	"	"
BG007	BG	MoEW	Recipient								
BG008	BG	Switzerland	Donor	Bilateral	Biodiversity Conservation Programme (Bulgarian-Swiss).	Ongoing	0	0	Education/training	Institutional development	"
BG008	BG	Bulgaria	Recipient								
CH001	BG	Faculty of Forestry of the University	Recipient	Bilateral	Sustainable forest management - Bulgaria	Completed	1996	2000	Capacity building	Policy/strategy	Know-how transfer
CH001	BG	Committee of Forests	Recipient	Bilateral	Sustainable forest management - Bulgaria	Completed	1996	2000	Capacity building	Policy/strategy	Know-how transfer
CH003	BG		Recipient	Bilateral	Effects of pollution on the ecosystems of forests -- Bulgaria	Completed	1997	2000	Technical development	Scientific/research	"

H3 Projects, Recipient Country: *Bulgaria (continued)*

Project ID		Organization	Position	Cooperation	Title	Status	From/in	To	Type 1	Type 2	Type 3
DE008	BG	Forest University	Recipient	Bilateral	Tissue culture of deciduous forest tree species	Completed	1995	1995	Education/training	Know-how transfer	
DE013	DE	Committee of Forest	Recipient	Bilateral	Exchange of experiences and advice of Bulgarian forest administration	Completed	1992	1995	Study tour	Know-how transfer	
DE079	BG	Committee of Forest	Recipient	Bilateral	Information on modern forest management	Completed	1992	0	Study tour	Know-how transfer	
DE084	GF	Ministry of Agriculture and Food Industry	Recipient	Bilateral	General support of the Bulgarian Government	Ongoing	0	0	Know-how transfer		
DE091	BG	Min. of Agriculture and Food Industry	Recipient	Bilateral	General support of the Bulgarian Government	Completed	1996	0	Education/training	Know-how transfer	
DE096	CH	Committee of Forests	Recipient	Bilateral	Counselling and know-how transfer with Bulgarian Committee of Forestry	Completed	1996	1997	Study tour	Seminar/workshop	Know-how transfer
DE107	BG	Staatliches Forstkomitee	Recipient	Bilateral	Training in the forest administration of Niedersachsen	Completed	1996	0	Seminar/workshop	Know-how transfer	
EU001	BG	MoEW (National Nature protection Service)mS. mlRA mlLEVA	Recipient	Multilateral	Sustainable forestry and forest biodiversity conservation in central-eastern Europe	Completed	1997	1998	Scientific/research	Capacity building	Policy/strategy
FO006	BG	Institute of Zoology, Academy of Science	Recipient	Multilateral	IUFRO/SPDC travel grants	Completed	1995	0	Other (travel grant)		
FR002	BG	University	Recipient	Multilateral	Technical and scientific cooperation in forestry reserch.	Completed	1993	1996	Scientific/research		
FR013	BG	Comité des Forêts Bulgare	Recipient	Bilateral	Expertise and training in strategic analysis and information technology in Bulgaria	Completed	1995	0	Know-how transfer		
GB012	BG	Municipality of Kurdjali	Recipient	Bilateral	Formulation of a strategy for the development of tourism	Completed	1995	0	Know-how transfer		
GR003	BG		Recipient	Bilateral	Scientific and Technical Cooperation	In planning	1995	1996	Scientific/research		

H3 Projects, Recipient Country: *Belarus*

Project ID		Organization	Position	Cooperation	Title	Status	From/in	To	Type 1	Type 2	Type 3
DE038	BY	WeiBruss, Staatliche Wissenschaftsunj	Recipient	Bilateral	Utilization of Lignin	Completed	1995	1996	Scientific/research	Know-how transfer	
DE040	BY	University Minsk	Recipient	Bilateral	Study on potential use of dendro volume for energy	In planning	1994	0	Scientific/research		
DE082	BY	Forest Administration of Belorussia	Recipient	Bilateral	Study Tour Forestry	Completed	0	0	Study tour		
DE101	BY	Moskauer Staatsuniversität des Waldes	Recipient	Bilateral	Long term development in requirements on power saws in Belarus.		1995	0	Scientific/research		
DK027	BY		Recipient	Bilateral	An Integrated Control Programme for Lymantria monacha in Belarus Forests for 1995	Completed	1995	1995	Scientific/research		
DK028	BY		Recipient	Trilateral	An Integrated Control Programme for Lymantria monacha and Dendrolemus Pini in Belarus Forest for 1996	Completed	1996	1996	Scientific/research		
DK031	BY		Recipient	Trilateral	Power Production from Radioactive Contaminated Biomass and Forest Litter in Belarus	Completed	1997	0	Technical development	Scientific/research	
FI001	BY	Belgosles (Ministry of Forestry)	Recipient	Trilateral	Forestry Strategic Plan, Belarus	Completed	1995	1997	Capacity building	Policy/strategy	

H3 Projects, Recipient Country: *Belarus (continued)*

Project ID		Organization	Position	Cooperation	Title	Status	From/in	To	Type 1	Type 2	Type 3
FI002	BY	Ministry of Forestry, Project Implementing Unit	Recipient	Multilateral	GIS Consultancy in Belarus	Completed	1995	0	Know-how transfer		
FI003	BY	Ministry of Forestry	Recipient	Bilateral	Forestry Specialist Course	In planning	1991	2005	Education/training	Know-how transfer	
GB033	BY		Recipient	Bilateral	Teacher Training Programme for permaculture practioners	Completed	2000	0	Study tour	Seminar/workshop	
PL006	BY	Forest Institute of Bas	Recipient	Multilateral	Lymantriamonacha (nun moth) control treatment	Suggested	1996	1997	Scientific/research	Capacity building	
PL009	BY	Byelarussin Academy of Science, Forest Institute	Recipient	Multilateral	Genetic diversity of forest tree species in central Europe	Suggested	1996	1998	Scientific/research		

H3 Projects, Recipient Country: *Croatia*

Project ID		Organization	Position	Cooperation	Title	Status	From/in	To	Type 1	Type 2	Type 3
AT005	HR	Ministry of Agriculture and Forestry	Recipient	Bilateral	Study Tour--Forest policy in Austria	Completed	1994	0	Study tour		
AT009	HR	Ministry of Agriculture & Forestry, Hrvatske Sume, Direkcija Zagreb	Recipient	Bilateral	Study Tour--Public forests in Austria	Completed	1995	0	Study tour		
DE073	HR	EUFORGEN	Recipient	Multilateral	EUROPGEN IPGRI Meeting on Hardwoods	Completed	1996	0	Seminar/workshop	Scientific/research	Know-how transfer
HR001	FA	Food and Agriculture Organization of the United Nations	Donor	Multilateral	Coastel forest reconstruction and protection project	In planning	1996	2000	Scientific/research		
HR001	HR	Croatian Forests	Recipient								
HR001	WB	World Bank	Donor								
HR001	HR	Government of Croatia	Donor								
HR001	HR	Forest Research Institute	Recipient								
HR002	HR	Ministry of Science and Technology	Donor	Bilateral	The development of new production management in wood processing and furniture manufacturing	Completed	1997	2000	Scientific/research		
HR002	HR	Ministry of Science and technology	Recipient								
HR003	HR	Ministry of Science and Technology	Donor	Bilateral	Eco-system management in wood processing	In planning	1999	2002	Scientific/research		
HR003	HR	Ministry of Science and Technology	Recipient								
HR003	SI		Donor								
HR003	SI		Recipient								

H3 Projects, Recipient Country: *Czech Republic*

Project ID		Organization	Position	Cooperation	Title	Status	From/in	To	Type 1	Type 2	Type 3
AT006	CZ	Vedouci obl. inspektoratu	Recipient	Bilateral	Study Tour--Austrian Torrent and Avalanche System	Completed	1994	0	Study tour		
AT020	CZ	Stredni Lesnicka Skola	Recipient	Bilateral	Study Tour--Students' exchange programme	Completed	1997	0	Study tour	Other	
AT033	CZ		Recipient	Bilateral	Study Tour--Forestry-related regional planning	Completed	1995	0	Study tour		
AT034	CZ		Recipient	Bilateral	Study Tour--Forestry-related regional planning	Completed	1995	0	Study tour		
AT035	CZ		Recipient	Bilateral	Study Tour--Recreation function of forests.	Completed	1995	0	Study tour		

H3 Projects, Recipient Country: *Czech Republic (continued)*

Project ID		Organization	Position	Cooperation	Title	Status	From/in	To	Type 1	Type 2	Type 3
AT036	CZ		Recipient	Bilateral	Study Tour--Forest management in mountainous areas	Completed	1995	0	Study tour		
AT037	CZ		Recipient	Bilateral	Study Tour--Protection of forests	Completed	1995	0	Study tour		
AT039	CZ		Recipient	Bilateral	Study tour--Forest management	Completed	1996	0	Study tour		
AT040	CZ		Recipient	Bilateral	Study Tour on Forest protection in mountainous areas.	Completed	1996	0	Study tour	Know-how transfer	
AT041	CZ		Recipient	Bilateral	Study Tour on Management of public forests	Completed	1996	0	Study tour		
AT042	CZ		Recipient	Bilateral	Study Tour on Protection function of forests	Completed	1996	0	Study tour		
AT043	CZ		Recipient	Bilateral	Study Tour on Forest management in private forests	Completed	1997	0	Study tour		
AT044	CZ		Recipient	Bilateral	Study Tour on Forestry and tourism	Completed	1997	0	Study tour		
AT045	CZ		Recipient	Bilateral	Study Tour on Management of protection of forests	Completed	1997	0	Study tour		
CZ001	EC	UNited Nations Economic Commission for Europe	Donor	Multilateral	Organization of 11th TFM of ICP-Forests	Completed	1995	0	Other (task force meeting		
CZ001	CZ	Ministry of Agriculture, Forestry Research Institute	Donor								
CZ002	CZ	Ministry of Agriculture, Forestry Research Institute	Donor	Multilateral	Forest seed collection, treatment and storage	Completed	1995	0	Seminar/workshop		
CZ003	WB	World Bank	Donor	Multilateral	Forest ecosystem restoration	Completed	1995	0	Seminar/workshop		
CZ003	CZ	Forestry Research Institute	Donor								
CZ004	DE	GSF Forschungzentrum	Donor	Trilateral	EU-Interreg-II: Case study BEECH in CZ/AT/Bavaria	Completed	1995	1998	Scientific/research		
CZ004	AT	Boku Vienna	Donor								
CZ004	CZ	FGMRI Jiloviste Strnady	Donor								
CZ005	SE	Göteborg University	Donor	Bilateral	Pheromone field tests of IPS-species	In planning	1996	1997	Education/training	Scientific/research	
CZ005	CZ	Forest Research Institute	Recipient								
CZ006	CH	WSL- Federal Research Institute	Donor	Bilateral	Migration in bark beetles and the efficiency of pheromone traps	Completed	1995	0	Education/training	Scientific/research	
CZ006	CZ	Forest Research Institute	Recipient								
CZ007	WB	World Bank	Donor	Bilateral	GEFI--Restoration of forest ecosystems	Completed	1996	0	Scientific/research	Technical development	
CZ007	CZ	FGMRI Jiloviste-Strnady	Recipient								
CZ008	WB	World Bank	Donor	Bilateral	GEF Biodiversity--Restoration of forests	Completed	1996	0	Scientific/research	Policy/strategy	Know-how transfer
CZ008	CZ	FGMRI Jiloviste-Strnady	Recipient								
CZ009	EU	EC -- Phare	Donor	Multilateral	Sustainable forestry and forest biodiversity conservation in central-eastern Europe	Completed	1998	2001	Policy/strategy	Scientific/research	
CZ009	CZ	Ministry of Agriculture	Recipient								
CZ010	CZ	Ministry of Agriculture	Recipient	Multilateral	Czech forestry sector study	Completed	1994	1995	Policy/strategy		
CZ010	EU	EC -- Phare	Donor								
CZ011	EC	UN-Economic Commission for Europe (ICP-F)	Donor	Multilateral	Workshop on level II--Forest health monitoring	Completed	1996	0	Seminar/workshop	Education/training	

H3 Projects, Recipient Country: *Czech Republic (continued)*

Project ID		Organization	Position	Cooperation	Title	Status	From/in	To	Type 1	Type 2	Type 3
CZ011	CZ	Forestry and Game Management Research Institute	Donor								
CZ012	CZ	Forest Research Institute	Donor	Multilateral	Forest tree seed pathology meeting	Completed	1996	0	Seminar/workshop		
CZ012	CZ	ISTA Tree Seed Pathology Committee	Donor								
CZ012	FA	IPGRI, Rome	Donor								
CZ013	FO	IUFRO, SPDC	Donor								
CZ013	CZ	Forestry & Game Management Res. Institute	Recipient								
CZ014	CZ	Forestry & Game Management Research Institute	Donor	Multilateral	Monitoring, research and management of ecosystems in the Krkonose National Park region	Completed	1996	0	Conference		
CZ014	CZ		Recipient	Multilateral	Monitoring, research and management of ecosystems in the Krkonose National Park region	Completed	1996	0	Conference		
CZ015	CZ	Forestry & Game Management Research Institute	Donor	Multilateral	Workshop on forest insect and disease survey	Completed	1997	0	Seminar/workshop		
CZ015	FO	IUFRO	Donor								
CZ016	CZ	Forestry and Game Management Research Institute, Jiloviste-Strnady	Donor	Multilateral	Workshop on "Importance of Research for Teaching and Everyday Life in Forestry"	Completed	1998	0	Seminar/workshop		
CZ016	CZ		Recipient								
CZ017	EC	UN/ECE Timber Committee and European Forestry Commission	Donor	Multilateral	Forest Certification and Countries in Transition	Completed	1998	1998	Seminar/workshop		
CZ017	CZ	Ministry of Agriculture of the Czech Republic	Donor								
CZ017	CZ		Recipient								
CZ017	CZ	Forestry and Game Management Research Institute, Jiloviste-Strnady	Donor								
CZ018	CZ	Forestry and Game Management Research Insitute, Jiloviste-Strnady	Recipient	Multilateral	The 3rd meeting of Picea abies EUFORGEN Network (EUFORGEN: European Forest Genetic Resources Programme)	Completed	1998	0	Seminar/workshop		
CZ019	CZ	Forestry and Game Management Research Institute, Jiloviste-Strnady	Recipient	Multilateral	Joint International Calibration Training Cource on Crown Assessment for Central and Eastern Europe	Completed	1997	0	Education/training		
CZ020	SE	SIDA	Donor	Bilateral	Forest Policy and State Forest Administration in Sweden	Completed	1997	0	Seminar/workshop		
CZ020	CZ		Recipient	Bilateral		Completed	1997	0	Seminar/workshop		

H3 Projects, Recipient Country: Czech Republic (continued)

Project ID		Organization	Position	Cooperation	Title	Status	From/in	To	Type 1	Type 2	Type 3
CZ020	SE	National Board of Forestry	Donor	Bilateral		Completed	1997	0	Seminar/workshop		
CZ021	FI	European Forest Institute	Donor	Multilateral	Conference on Forest policy in Countries with Economies in Transition - "ready for the European Union?"	Completed	1997	0	Conference		
CZ021	CZ	Forestry and Game Management Research Institute	Recipient								
CZ021	CZ	Ministry of Agriculture of the Czech Republic	Recipient								
CZ021	CZ	Czech University of Agriculture, Faculty of Forestry,	Recipient								
CZ021	CZ		Donor								
CZ022	CZ	Institute for Forest Ecosystem Research (IFER)	Recipient	Multilateral	Atmospheric Deposition and Forest Management	Completed	1996	0	Seminar/workshop		
CZ022	NL	Institute for Forestry and Nature Research (IBN-DLO)	Donor								
CZ022	NL	NATO-ARW, Min. of Agriculture/Min. of Environment	Donor								
CZ023	US	Czechoslovak Science and Technology Program	Donor	Bilateral	Forest health monitoring - Assessment of ozone concentration and its phytotoxicity in the Czech Republic	Completed	1996	0	Scientific/research		
CZ023	CZ	Institute for Forest Ecosystem Research (IFER)	Recipient								
CZ023	US	USAD Forest Service, Foresst Fire Laboratory	Donor								
CZ024	CZ	Institute for Forest Ecosystem Research (IFER)	Recipient	Bilateral	Forest damage and related environmental factors in the Krkonose Mts.	Completed	1997	0	Scientific/research		
CZ024	CZ	The Krkonose National Park	Recipient								
CZ025	SK	Slovak Academy of Sciences, Institute of Landscape Ecology	Recipient	Multilateral	Evaluation of ozone air pollution and its phytotoxic potential in the Carpathian forests	Completed	1997	0	Scientific/research		
CZ025	FO	IUFRO Special Programme for developing countries	Donor								
CZ025	CZ	Institute for Forest Ecosystem Research (IFER)	Recipient								
CZ025	US	USDA Forest Service, Forest Fire Laboratory, USA	Donor								

H3 Projects, Recipient Country: *Czech Republic (continued)*

Project ID		Organization	Position	Cooperation	Title	Status	From/in	To	Type 1	Type 2	Type 3
CZ025	PL	Polish Academy of Sciences, Institute of Botany	Recipient								
CZ026	UA	Ukrainian Research Inst. of Forestry	Recipient	Multilateral	Scenario analysis of sustainable wood production under different forest management regimes	Ongoing	1998	2001	Scientific/research		
CZ026	FI	European Forest Institute	Recipient								
CZ026	PL	Forest Research Institute	Recipient								
CZ026	CZ	Institute for Forest Ecosystem Research (IFER)	Recipient								
CZ026	HU	State Forest Service	Recipient								
CZ026	NL	Institute for Forestry and Nature Research	Recipient								
CZ027	WB	World Bank	Donor	Multilateral	GEF I - Restoration of Forest Ecosystems--Global Environment Facility/Biodiversity Protection Project	Completed	1993	1997	Education/training	Financial assistance	Capacity building
CZ027	CZ	Ministry of Environment and Forestry Dept. of Min. of Agriculture	Recipient								
CZ027	EP	United Nations Env. Programme	Donor								
CZ027	UA		Recipient								
CZ028	FO	IUFRO Region 2 - Central Europe and IUFRO Division 6	Donor	Bilateral	Seminar on "Forestry Research on the Threshold of the 3rd Millennium"	Completed	1998	0	Seminar/workshop		
CZ028	CZ	Ministry of Agriculture and Forestry and Game Management Research Institute of the CZ	Donor								
CZ028	CZ		Recipient								
CZ029	CZ	Czech experts	Recipient	Bilateral	Project on "Reproduction of mature elm trees using in vitro methods" under European Cooperation in Science and Technology programme.	Ongoing	1997	2001	Scientific/research		
CZ030	NL	Dutch Foundation (FACE)	Donor	Bilateral	Genetic studies in the Krkonose National Park in Czech Republic	Completed	1997	0			
CZ030	CZ		Recipient								
CZ031	CZ		Recipient	Multilateral	Reproduction of mature elm trees using in vitro methods (COST822 50/1997)	Completed	0	2000			
CZ033	CZ	Forest Research Institute	Recipient	Bilateral	Bilateral collaboration of Forest Research Institute with NE Forest Exp. Station of USDA in forest protection		0	0			
CZ033	US	NE Forest Exp. Station of USDA	Donor	Bilateral	Bilateral collaboration of Forest Research Institute with NE Forest Exp. Station of USDA in forest protection		0	0			

H3 Projects, Recipient Country: *Czech Republic (continued)*

Project ID		Organization	Position	Cooperation	Title	Status	From/in	To	Type 1	Type 2	Type 3
CZ034	CZ		Recipient		Strengthening of private andcommunity forestry in Central and Eastern Europe	In planning	0	0	0		
CZ034	FA	FAO	Donor								
CZ035	CZ		Partner		COST E19, NFP	In planning	0	0	0	″	″
CZ036	CZ		Partner		Round Table on Management of Mountain Watersheds, Prague	Completed	0	2001	Conference		″
CZ037	CZ		Partner		Seminar on Valuation of Forest Goods and Service, Opocno, November 2000.	Completed	0	0	0	″	″
CZ038	CZ		Partner		International workshop of IUFRO WG of Division 3, Methodology of forest pests and diseases assessment, Prague.	In planning	0	2002	″	″	″
CZ039	CZ		Partner		Forest Entomological Congress, 2002	In planning	0	0	0	″	″
CZ040	CZ		Partner		Study tour in the frame of IYM, EOMF activity, Northern and Eastern Bohemia, June 2002	In planning	0	0	0	″	″
DE002	CZ	Forest Management Institute	Recipient	Bilateral	Monitoring of Forest Damage in the Erzgebirge and the Fichtelgebirge by means of remote sensing	Completed	1993	1996	Scientific/research		
DE003	CZ	Ministerstvo Zemedelstri Sächs	Donor	Trilateral	"Black Triangle" Schwarzes Dreieck--Specific working group forest protection and hunting	Completed	1993	0	Study tour	Policy/strategy	Know-how transfer
DE006	CZ	Skolni Lesni Podnik	Recipient	Bilateral	Training in grafting methods	Completed	1995	0	Education/training		
DE007	CZ	Forest Tree Nursery Olesna	Recipient	Bilateral	In vitro culture technique forest species	Completed	1995	1995	Scientific/research	Know-how transfer	
DE009	CZ	Forestry Nursery Olesna	Recipient	Bilateral	Evolution of Picea hybrids in field trials	Completed	1995	0	Scientific/research		
DE035	CZ	Les projekt, Brandys n.L.	Recipient	Multilateral	Forest condition assessment in the Fichtelgebirge and mountains using remote sensing	Completed	1993	1996	Scientific/research		
DE050	CZ	Forestry and Game Management Research Institute	Recipient	Multilateral	Case study on common beech in the Bohemian, Czech and Bavaria triangle	Completed	1995	1997	Scientific/research		
DE059	CZ	Forestry and Game Management Research Inst.	Recipient	Multilateral	Differential diagnosing of oak damage in the Danub region	Completed	1992	1994	Scientific/research		
DE060	CZ	Forest Planning Institute UHUL-LES-Projekt	Recipient	Bilateral	Forest damage assessment in the Fichtelgebirge and ore mountains utility remote sensing techniques	Completed	1993	1996	Scientific/research		
DE063	CZ	Londw. Univ. BRNO, Dept. of Silviculture	Donor	Multilateral	Joint workshops BRNO-THARANDT	Ongoing	0	0	Seminar/workshop	Seminar/workshop	
DE073	CZ	VULHM, Jiloviste-Strnady	Recipient	Multilateral	EUROPGEN IPGRI Meeting on Hardwoods	Completed	1996	0	Seminar/workshop	Scientific/research	Know-how transfer
DE073	CZ	VULHM, Jiloviste-Strnady	Recipient	Multilateral	EUROPGEN IPGRI Meeting on Hardwoods	Completed	1996	0	Seminar/workshop	Scientific/research	Know-how transfer
DE074	CZ	Landwirtschaftliche Hochschule, Forstl. Fakultat	Recipient	Bilateral	Practical training for forestry students	Completed	1996	0	Education/training	Scientific/research	Know-how transfer
DE076	CZ	Landwirtschaftministerium	Recipient	Bilateral	Organization of forestry in Germany	Completed	1996	0	Study tour		

H3 Projects, Recipient Country: *Czech Republic (continued)*

Project ID		Organization	Position	Cooperation	Title	Status	From/in	To	Type 1	Type 2	Type 3
DE081	CZ	Federal Forest Administration	Recipient	Bilateral	Natural forest economy	Completed	0	0	Seminar/workshop	Education/training	
DE094	CZ	Forestry and Game Management	Recipient	Trilateral	Physiological and phenological analysis of beech in two altitudes on the bavarian plots	Completed	1995	1997	Scientific/research		
DE095	CZ	Czech Forest Administration	Recipient	Bilateral	Special tours of Czech forest experts	Completed	0	0	Study tour	Know-how transfer	
DE109	CZ	Forstverwaltung of Czech Rep., Inst. vychovy a vdelavani,	Recipient	Bilateral	Stage and cooperation forest administration of Czech Republic	In planning	0	0	Know-how transfer		
DE147	CZ	Czech Ministry of agriculture	Recipient	Bilateral	Training in harvesting of Timber	Completed	2001	0	Education/training		"
EF001	CZ		Recipient	Multilateral	Growth Trend of European Forests	Completed	1996	0	Scientific/research		
EP001	CZ	Ministry of Agriculture	Recipient	Multilateral	Support to policy and guidelines for sustainable management of temperate forest ecosystems *	Completed	1994	1995	Policy/strategy		
EU001	CZ	Forest and Soil Protection Dept. Min. of the Environment	Recipient	Multilateral	Sustainable forestry and forest biodiversity conservation in central-eastern Europe	Completed	1998	2001	Scientific/research	Capacity building	Policy/strategy
FO001	CZ	University of Agriculture, Faculty of Forestry	Recipient	Multilateral	IUFRO/SPDC Travel grants	Completed	1994	0	Seminar/workshop	Other(travel grant)	
FO001	CZ	Forestry and Game Management Research Institute	Recipient	Multilateral	IUFRO/SPDC Travel grants	Completed	1994	0	Seminar/workshop	Other(travel grant)	
FO007	CZ	Forestry and Game Management Institute	Recipient	Multilateral	IUFRO/SPDC travel grants	Completed	1995	0	Other (travel grant)		
FR004	CZ	Forestry and Game Management Research Institute, VULHM	Recipient	Trilateral	Technical and scientific cooperation in forestry research	Completed	1994	1997	Scientific/research		
GB027	CZ		Recipient	Multilateral	PhD Scholarship (Wiliam M. Barrett)	Completed	2000	0	Scientific/research		"
GB031	CZ		Recipient	Trilateral	Free and Applied Internships on "Renewables & Efficiency" Training and Internship Programme	Completed	1999	0	Seminar/workshop	Education/training	Know-how transfer
GB035	CZ		Recipient	Bilateral	Seminar course in "new economics" aimed at Czech/Slovak NGOs focussing on grass-roots development and the environment	Completed	2000	0	Seminar/workshop		"
GR002	CZ		Recipient	Bilateral	Scientific and Technical Cooperation	In planning	1995	1996	Scientific/research		
SE002	CZ		Recipient	Trilateral	Study tour on "Evaluation of forest"	Completed	1995	0	Study tour		
SE003	CZ	Ministry of Forestry Prage	Recipient	Bilateral	Forest policy, legislation and extension	Completed	1995	0	Know-how transfer		
SE027	CZ	Ministry of Agriculture	Recipient	Bilateral	Study tour to follow-up of the two courses on "Training, Information in Estonia" and "Forest Mensuration and Evaluation" carried out in 1995.	Completed	1997	1997	Study tour	Education/training	"
UA005	CZ		Donor	Multilateral	Effects of Air Pollution on Forests Health and Biodiversity in forests of the Carpathian Mountains (Programme of IUFRO-SPDC)	Completed	1997	2001	Scientific/research		"

H3 Projects, Recipient Country: Czech Republic (continued)

Project ID		Organization	Position	Cooperation	Title	Status	From/in	To	Type 1	Type 2	Type 3
UA009	CZ		Donor	Multilateral	Scenario analysis of sustainable wood production under different forest management regimes (SCEFORMA) (INCO-Copernicus programme)	Ongoing	1998	2001	Education/training	Technical assistance	"

H3 Projects, Recipient Country: *Estonia*

Project ID		Organization	Position	Cooperation	Title	Status	From/in	To	Type 1	Type 2	Type 3
DE032	EE	State Forest Service	Recipient	Bilateral	Support of Estonian State Forest Service	Completed	1994		Education/training	Know-how transfer	
DE033	EE	State Forest Service	Recipient	Bilateral	Support of Estonian State Forest Service	Completed	1995		Study tour	Know-how transfer	
DE051	EE	University	Recipient	Bilateral	Dendrochronology	Completed	1995	0	Scientific/research		
DE070	EE	Estonian Forest Research Institute	Recipient	Bilateral	Ecological and economical constraints of natural and afforested pine stands in Estonia	In planning	1996	1998	Scientific/research		
DE070	EE	Estonian Agricultural University, Forestry Dept., Univ. of Tartu	Recipient	Bilateral	Ecological and economical constraints of natural and afforested pine stands in Estonia	In planning	1996	1998	Scientific/research		
DE085	EE	State Forest Service	Recipient	Bilateral	Support of Estonian State Forest Service	Ongoing	0	0	Know-how transfer		
DE099	EE	University of Tartu	Recipient	Bilateral	Exchange of students of wood science and technology and wood economy.	Completed	1994	0	Study tour		
DK002	EE	Luua Korgen Mesakool	Recipient	Multilateral	Development of Luua, Foretry College, Estonia	In planning	1995	1996	Study tour	Seminar/workshop	Know-how transfer
DK008	EE	Estonian Forest Department	Recipient	Bilateral	Institutional Support and Infrastructural Development Programme for the Estonian Forest Department	Completed	1994	1995	Know-how transfer		
DK009	EE	Estonian State Forest Dept. and Forest Faculty at the University of Tartu	Recipient	Bilateral	Support for establishment of supplementary education facility at Tartu, Estonia	Completed	1995	1996	Know-how transfer		
DK012	EE		Recipient	Bilateral	A Sustainable Management Strategy for Estonien Forested Wetlands	Completed	1997	1998	Policy/strategy		
DK038	EE		Recipient	Bilateral	Development of the Estonian Forest Area Network	Ongoing	0	0	Institutional development		
DK039	EE		Recipient	Bilateral	Protection of the Biodiversity of the Soomaa National Park	Completed	0	0	Technical assistance		
EE001	FI	INDUFOR	Donor	Bilateral	Estonian forestry development programme	Completed	0	0	Education/training	Scientific/research	Technical development
EE001	DK	Holstenburg	Donor								
EE001	SE		Donor								
EE001	EE	Forest Department	Recipient								
EE002	DK	Danish Environmental Protection Agency	Donor	Bilateral	Estonian forest conservation area network	Ongoing	1999	2001	Technical development	Policy/strategy	Know-how transfer
EE002	DK	Carol Bro International a/s	Donor								
EE002	EE	Ministry of Environment	Recipient								
EE003	SE	Country Forestry Board of Ostra Gotaland	Donor	Bilateral	Full-scale Woodland Key Habitat Inventory in Estonia	Ongoing	1999	2002	Scientific/research		
EE003	SE	Swedish Environmental Protection Agency	Donor								

H3 Projects, Recipient Country: *Estonia (continued)*

Project ID		Organization	Position	Cooperation	Title	Status	From/in	To	Type 1	Type 2	Type 3
EE003	EE	Ministry of Environment	Recipient		Establishment of demonstration areas to illustrate ways and means of forest management practices and planning.	In planning	0	0	Education/training	Scientific/research	
EE004	EE	Ministry of Environment	Recipient	Multilateral							
EE004	EE	Private Forest Centre	Recipient								
EE004	FI	Forestry Development Centre Tapio	Donor								
EE005	FI	Central Union of Agricultural Producers and Forest Owners MTK	Donor	Bilateral	Promoting sustainable forest management in Estonian private forests by forest certification.	In planning	2000	2000	Education/training	Capacity building	Know-how transfer
EE005	FI	Family Timber Finland	Donor								
EE005	EE	Private Forest Centre	Recipient								
EE006	SE	National Board of Forestry, Sweden	Donor	Bilateral	Estonian and Swedish cooperational project about deciduous forests sustainable management	Completed	1998	2000	Seminar/workshop	Know-how transfer	
EE006	EE	Ministry of Environment	Recipient								
EE006	EE	AS Sylvester	Recipient								
EE007	EU	European Community, Phar/Tacis CBC Project facility	Donor	Bilateral	Establishment of foundation Private Forest Centre	Completed	1998	2000	Seminar/workshop	Education/training	
EE007	EE	Ministry of Environment	Recipient								
EE008	FI		Donor		The Hybrid Aspen project		0	0	Scientific/research		
EE008	EE		Recipient								
EE009	EE		Donor		Meeting of Forestry Societies of Baltic States, Sagadi, Estonia (15-16 August 2001	Completed	2001	2001	Seminar/workshop		
EE010	EE		Recipient		Reconstruction of wooded meadows and pastures in Saaremaa		0	0	Scientific/research	Technical assistance	Capacity building
EE010	FI		Donor								
EE010	SE		Donor								
EE011	EE		Donor		The Baltic 21 Forest Sector Meeting, Sagadi, Estonia, held on 26-28.09 2001	Completed	2001	2001	Policy/strategy		
EU001	EE	Ministry of Environment	Recipient	Multilateral	Sustainable forestry and forest biodiversity conservation in central-eastern Europe	Completed	1998	2001	Scientific/research	Capacity building	Policy/strategy
FA002	EE		Donor	Multilateral	Development of marketing of sawnwood products in countries in transition to market economies	Completed	1995	0	Seminar/workshop	Capacity building	
FI004	EE	Estonian Forestry Department	Recipient	Multilateral	Estonian Forestry Development Programme (EFDP)	Completed	1995	1998	Capacity building	Policy/strategy	Know-how transfer
FI005	EE		Recipient	Bilateral	Expert seminar on the establishment of a site information system in the Baltic region	Completed	1995	0	Seminar/workshop		
FI007	EE	Eesti Riigi Maa-amet	Recipient	Bilateral	Assistance in land reform in Estonia	Completed	1992	1995	Technical development	Capacity building	Know-how transfer
FI008	EE	Estonian Forestry Department	Recipient	Bilateral	Development of private forest economy in Estonia	Completed	1992	1995	Capacity building	Know-how transfer	
FI009	EE	Viko A/S	Recipient	Bilateral	Valga Sawmill in Estonia	Completed	1994	1995	Capacity building	Know-how transfer	
FI010	EE		Recipient	Bilateral	Delivering a circular saw to Võru in Estonia	Completed	1994	1995	Technical development	Know-how transfer	

H3 Projects, Recipient Country: *Estonia (continued)*

Project ID		Organization	Position	Cooperation	Title	Status	From/in	To	Type 1	Type 2	Type 3
FI011	EE	Forest Department	Recipient	Bilateral	Development of forest statistics in the Baltic countries (feasibility study)	Completed	1995	0	Scientific/research		
FI012	EE	Luua College of Forestry	Recipient	Bilateral	Forestry training development project in Estonia	Completed	1993	1995	Education/training	Capacity building	Know-how transfer
FI012	EE	Rápina College of Forestry	Recipient	Bilateral	Forestry training development project in Estonia	Completed	1993	1995	Education/training	Capacity building	Know-how transfer
FI013	EE	Rápina College of Forestry	Recipient	Bilateral	Development project of education in Estonian sawmilling industry	Completed	1995	0	Education/training	Know-how transfer	
FI014	EE	Estonian Agricultural University	Recipient	Bilateral	Education of Baltic experts, adaptation of the Finnish MELA-system for forestry analysis in Baltic countries	Completed	1995	1996	Scientific/research	Capacity building	Know-how transfer
FI018	EE		Recipient	Multilateral	Establishment and start-up of the Baltic Environmental Education Network	Completed	1995	0	Seminar/workshop	Education/training	
GB009	EE	Lahemaa National park	Recipient	Bilateral	Visit by Estonian Foresters	Completed	1995	0	Study tour		
GB011	EE	Tartu University, Forestry Department	Recipient	Bilateral	Estonian students forestry tour	Completed	1995	0	Study tour	Education/training	
GB029	EE		Recipient	Bilateral	Baltic States Rural Development Project	Ongoing	2000	2003	Know-how transfer		
NO004	EE	UPA College of Agriculture	Recipient	Bilateral	Forest Education at UPA College of Agriculture, Estonia	Completed	1995	0	Education/training		
SE001	EE	Estonian Agricultural University	Recipient	Bilateral	Study tour on "Fuel energy"	Completed	1995	1995	Study tour	Seminar/workshop	
SE010	EE		Recipient	Bilateral	Training course on "Forest management in a market economy"	Completed	1993	0	Education/training		
SE016	EE	Estonian Elementary Schools	Recipient	Bilateral	Exchange programme "Forest at school"	Completed	1994	0	Education/training		
SE020	EE	Estonian schools	Recipient	Bilateral	Training course on general forestry training to Estonian teachers	Completed	1996	1996	Seminar/workshop	Policy/strategy	
SE021	EE	Estonian Forest Department	Recipient	Bilateral	Training course on information on forest policy and environmental consideration	Completed	1996	1996	Seminar/workshop	Policy/strategy	
SE022	EE	Estonian Agricultureal University	Recipient	Bilateral	Study tour on "Domestic Energy Resources"	Completed	1997	1997	Study tour		
SE023	EE	Estonian Forest Department	Recipient	Bilateral	Training of Forestry Extension Agents	Completed	1997	1998	Education/training	Capacity building	
SE029	EE		Recipient	Bilateral	Key habitat inventories -- a project in Estonia, Latvia, Lithuania.	Ongoing	1999	2004			
SE031	EE		Recipient	Bilateral	Green Forest Management Planning -- a project in Estonia	Completed	2001	2002			

H3 Projects, Recipient Country: *Hungary*

Project ID		Organization	Position	Cooperation	Title	Status	From/in	To	Type 1	Type 2	Type 3
AT028	HU	Hungarian Foresters Association	Recipient	Trilateral	Study Tour--Pannonia Meeting 1996	Completed	1996	0	Study tour		
CZ026	HU	State Forest Service	Recipient	Multilateral	Scenario analysis of sustainable wood production under different forest management regimes (SCEFORMA)	Ongoing	1998	2001	Scientific/research		
DE018	HU	University Sopron	Recipient	Multilateral	2nd International Conference on the development of wood science	In planning	1996	0	Seminar/workshop		

H3 Projects, Recipient Country: *Hungary (continued)*

Project ID		Organization	Position	Cooperation	Title	Status	From/in	To	Type 1	Type 2	Type 3
DE021	HU	Forstverwaltung, Ministerium für Landwirtschaft, Landesamt für Forstwesen	Recipient	Bilateral	Cooperation with the Hungarian Forest Authorities: President's visit	Completed	0	0	Study tour		
DE022	HU	Forstverwaltung, Ministerium für Landwirtschaft, Landesamt für Forstwesen	Recipient	Bilateral	Cooperation with Hungary - visit of foresters	Completed	1995	0	Education/training		
DE023	HU	Forstverwaltung, Universität für Forst-und Holzwissensohaften	Recipient	Bilateral	Cooperation with Hungary -- training of forestry students	Completed	1995	0	Education/training		
DE052	HU	University	Recipient	Multilateral	Technology for products from black locust (Robinia pseudoacacia)	Completed	1996	0	Scientific/research	Technical development	
DE059	HU	University of Forestry	Recipient	Multilateral	Differential diagnosing of oak damage in the Danub region	Completed	1992	1994	Scientific/research		
DE071	HU		Donor	Bilateral	Non-destructive testing in the timber section	Completed	1993	1998	Seminar/workshop	Scientific/research	Technical development
DE071	HU	Universität Sopron	Recipient								
DE092	HU	Universität Sopron	Recipient	Bilateral	Partnership University Freiburg - Sopron	Completed	1983	0	Education/training		
DE093	HU	University of Forest 1 Timber Science	Recipient	Bilateral	Training in forest management	In planning	0	0	Education/training		
DE093	HU	State Administration of Forest Management	Recipient								
DE105	HU	Landesamt für Forstwesen	Recipient	Bilateral	Training in the forest administration of Baden-Wurttemberg	Completed	1996	0	Seminar/workshop	Know-how transfer	
DE105	HU	Ministry of Agriculture	Recipient								
DE108	HU	Forstverwaltung Ministerium für Landwirtschaft - Landesamt für Forstwesen	Recipient	Bilateral	Stage and cooperation with Hungarian forest administration	Completed	0	0	Education/training		
DE117	HU	Ministry of Agriculture	Recipient	Bilateral	Forestry in Baden-Württemberg - assistance to Hungary	Completed	1997	1997	Study tour		
DE129	HU	Ministry of Agriculture	Recipient	Bilateral	Forestry in Baden-Württemberg	Completed	1999	1999	Study tour		
DE137	HU	Ministry of Agriculture	Recipient	Bilateral	Forestry in Baden-Württemberg - assistance to Hungary	In planning	2000	2000	Study tour		
EU001	HU	Min. of the Environment & Regional Policy, Dept. of N. P. & Forestry	Recipient	Multilateral	Sustainable forestry and forest biodiversity conservation in central-eastern Europe	Completed	1998	2001	Scientific/research	Capacity building	Policy/strategy
FO008	HU	University of Forestry and Wood Sciences	Recipient	Multilateral	IUFRO/SPDC travel grants	Completed	1995	0	Other (travel grants)		
FR003	HU	ERTI	Recipient	Bilateral	Technical and scientific cooperation in forestryresearch	Completed	1994	1999	Scientific/research		
FR010	HU		Recipient	Trilateral	Technical and scientific cooperation in forestry research	Completed	1990	1996	Scientific/research		

H3 Projects, Recipient Country: *Hungary (continued)*

Project ID		Organization	Position	Cooperation	Title	Status	From/in	To	Type 1	Type 2	Type 3
FR015	HU	Faipari Kutato Intezet	Recipient	Bilateral	Scientific and technological cooperation	Suggested	0	0	Scientific/research	Technical development	
FR016	HU	ERTI	Recipient	Bilateral	Support in favour of Hungarian private forest development	In planing	1996	1997	Technical development		
GB027	HU		Recipient	Multilateral	PhD Scholarship (Wiliam M. Barrelt)	Completed	2000	0	Scientific/research		
GB031	HU		Recipient	Trilateral	Free and Applied Internships on "Renewables & Efficiency" Training and Internship Programme	Completed	1999	0	Seminar/workshop	Education/training	Know-how transfer
HU001	EU	European Commission--Phare	Donor	Multilateral	Business analysis on strategic review of the Hungarian State Forestry Portfolio	Completed	1995	0	Policy/strategy	Other (Strategic study)	
HU001	HU	Ministry of Agriculture, Office for Forestry	Recipient								
HU002	HU	Hungarian Forest Association	Recipient	Bilateral	Study tour in Canada	Completed	1995	0	Study tour		
HU002	HU	Hungarian forest employers	Recipient								
HU002	HU	Hungarian forest employers	Donor								
HU003	HU	Ministry of Agriculture	Donor	Bilateral	Study tour in Germany	Completed	1995	0	Study tour		
HU003	HU	Hungarian Forest Association	Recipient								
HU003	DE	Ministry of Food, Agriculture and Forestry	Donor								
HU003	HU	Ministry of Agriculture	Recipient								
HU004	HU	Hungarian Forest Employers	Donor	Bilateral	Study tou in Slovenia	Completed	1995	0	Study tour		
HU004	SI	Slovenian Forestry Association	Donor								
HU004	HU	Hungary Forest Employers	Recipient								
HU004	HU	Hungary Forest Association	Recipient								
HU005	HU	Ministry of Agriculture	Donor	Multilateral	Participation in the 26the International Forest and Wood Industry Seminar, and sight of "Holzmess Klagenfurt 95"	Completed	1995	0	Seminar/workshop	Other (exhibition)	
HU005	HU	Ministry of Agriculture	Recipient								
HU006	HU	Ministry of Agriculture	Donor	Multilateral	Participation in the technical programe of LIGNA-Hannover'95 and Inter Holz'95	Completed	1995	0	Seminar/workshop	Other (exhibition)	
HU006	HU	Ministry of Agriculture	Recipient								
HU007	HU	Ministry of Agriculture	Donor	Multilateral	International Forestry Seminar on Exploring Multiple Use and Ecosystem Management	Completed	1995	0	Seminar/workshop		
HU007	CA	Forest Service	Donor								
HU008	HU	Ministry of Agriculture, Forest Office	Recipient	Bilateral	Functioning of the forest inspection system, forest inspection of the private forest management	Completed	1996	1997	Study tour	Capacity building	
HU008	AT		Donor								
HU009	HU	Ministry of Agriculture, Forest Office	Recipient	Bilateral	Subvention scheme of the private forest management	Completed	1996	1997	Study tour	Capacity building	

H3 Projects, Recipient Country: *Hungary (continued)*

Project ID		Organization	Position	Cooperation	Title	Status	From/in	To	Type 1	Type 2	Type 3
HU009	AT		Donor								
HU010	AT		Donor	Bilateral	Methods and results of the forest management, with special regard to the growth. Roadside plantation and regeneration on sodic soil.	Completed	1996	1997	Education/training		
HU010	HU	Ministry of Agriculture	Recipient								
HU011	AT		Donor	Bilateral	Molecular genetic analyses in form sphere of the poplars, identification of genotypes with molecular biological methods		0	0	Scientific/research	Technical assistance	
HU011	HU	Ministry of Agriculture	Recipient								
HU012	AT	Ministry of Agriculture	Donor	Bilateral	Spatial development planning for forestry	Completed	1996	1997	Study tour	Capacity building	
HU012	HU	Ministry of Agriculture	Recipient								
HU013	AT	Bundesministerium fur Land-und Forstwirtschaft	Donor	Bilateral	Consultation on INTERREG II. C. prlject in Vienna in the theme of spatial development planning for forestry.		0	0	Capacity building	Scientific/research	
HU013	AT	Bundesministerium fur Land-und Forstwirtschaft	Recipient								
HU013	HU	Ministry of Agriculture	Recipient								
HU013	HU	Ministry of Agriculture	Recipient								
HU014	DE	Baden-Württemberg	Donor	Bilateral	Afforestation, supporting and regulating systems, private forestry, planning and forest inspection system		0	0	Study tour	Capacity building	
HU014	HU	Ministry of Agriculture	Recipient								
HU015	DE	Baden-Württemberg	Donor	Bilateral	Controlling and supporting activity of the forest authority, special regard to private forest property.		0	0	Study tour	Capacity building	
HU015	HU	Ministry of Agriculture	Recipient								
HU016	DE	Baden-Württemberg	Donor	Bilateral	Different method of sylviculture (ecology-economics); application of computer technics in forest management (GIS, MTO).		0	0	Study tour	Capacity building	
HU016	HU	Ministry of Agriculture	Recipient								
HU017	HU	Ministry of Agriculture	Recipient	Bilateral	Forest management in broadleaved forest, transformation of pine stands for mixed broadleaved forest, near-to-nature forest management.		0	0	Study tour	Capacity building	
HU017	DE	Baden-Württemberg	Donor								
HU018	DE	Baden-Württemberg	Donor	Bilateral	Marketing activity, relations between different institutions, the trade and forest industries		0	0	Study tour	Capacity building	
HU018	HU	Ministry of Agriculture	Recipient								
HU019	DE	Baden-Württemberg	Donor	Bilateral	Silviculture, harvesting, game management		0	0	Study tour	Capacity building	
HU019	HU	Ministry of Agriculture	Recipient								
HU020	DE	Baden-Württemberg	Donor	Bilateral	Natural reforestation and thinning in broadleaved and pine stands		0	0	Study tour	Capacity building	
HU020	HU	Ministry of Agriculture	Recipient								
HU021	DE	Thüringer Ministerium für Landwirtschaft Naturschutz und Umvelt	Donor	Bilateral	Studying the Hungarian forest- and game management		0	0	Study tour		

H3 Projects, Recipient Country: *Hungary (continued)*

Project ID		Organization	Position	Cooperation	Title	Status	From/in	To	Type 1	Type 2	Type 3
HU021	HU	Ministry of Agriculture, Forest Office	Recipient								
HU022	DE	Bavaria Ministerium für Landwirtschaft	Donor	Bilateral	Studying the Hungarian forest- and game management.		0	0	Study tour		
HU022	HU	Ministry of Agriculture, Forest Office	Recipient								
HU023	GR		Donor	Multilateral	International project INTERREG II.C No. 97005/ "Natural Resources"	Completed	1999	2000	Policy/strategy		
HU023	HU		Donor								
HU023	DE		Donor								
HU023	AT		Donor								
HU024	HU		Recipient	Bilateral	Sylviculture questions of deciduous tree species, results and extension of forest genetic research	Completed	2000	2000	Scientific/research	Technical development	
HU024	AT		Donor								
HU025	AT		Donor	Bilateral	Diagnosis of nematod damage in coniferous forests and fungal diseases in alder forests	Completed	2000	2000	Scientific/research		
HU025	HU		Recipient								
HU026	AT		Donor	Bilateral	Information and support systems of Austrian private forestry	Completed	2000	2000	Study tour		
HU026	HU		Recipient								
HU027	HU		Recipient	Bilateral	Near-to-natrue forest management and means of forest management	Completed	2000	2000	Study tour	Capacity building	
HU027	AT		Donor								
HU028	AT		Donor	Bilateral	Tree harvesting technologies	Completed	2000	2000	Study tour	Capacity building	
HU028	HU		Recipient								
HU029	HU	State Forest Service	Recipient	Multilateral	Development of the forestry information system (HU-2001/IB/AG-02)	Ongoing	2002	2003	Capacity building	Institutional development	Technical development
HU029	DE	Bundesministerium für Agriculture ,Ernahrung und Verbrauchenschutz	Partner								
HU029	EU	Phare	Donor								
HU029	AT	Öbf AG	Partner								
HU030	EU	Phare	Donor	Multilateral	Wood Sector Study	Completed	1992	0	Policy/strategy		
HU030	HU	Min. of Agr.	Recipient								
HU031	EU	Phare	Donor	Multilateral	Wood Sector Study II	Completed	1993	0	Policy/strategy		
HU031	HU	Min. of Agr.	Recipient								
HU032	EU	Phare	Donor	Multilateral	Strategic Review (Forestry Portfolio Business Analysis)	Completed	1995	0	Policy/strategy		
HU032	HU		Recipient								
HU033	IE	Beltra Forestry Ltd.	Partner	Multilateral	The privatisation of forests in Hungary	Completed	1995	0	Policy/strategy		
HU033	HU	Min. of Agr.	Partner								
IE001	HU	Ministry of Agriculture	Recipient	Multilateral	Forestry portfolio business analysis and strategic review	Completed	1995	0	Policy/strategy	Institutional development	
IE007	HU	MAGOR	Recipient	Bilateral	MBA Thesis	Completed	1993	0	Education/training		

H3 Projects, Recipient Country: *Hungary (continued)*

Project ID		Organization	Position	Cooperation	Title	Status	From/in	To	Type 1	Type 2	Type 3
UA009	HU		Donor	Multilateral	Scenario analysis of sustainable wood production under different forest management regimes (SCEFORMA) (INCO-Copernicus programme)	Ongoing	1998	2001	Education/training	Technical assistance	
UA011	HU		Partner	Multilateral	Scientific background of reforestation and afforestation improvement activities in Carpathian mountains	Ongoing	2000	0	Scientific/research		

H3 Projects, Recipient Country: *Latvia*

Project ID		Organization	Position	Cooperation	Title	Status	From/in	To	Type 1	Type 2	Type 3
DE020	LV	Universität Jelgava	Recipient	Bilateral	Study tour for Latvian forestry students	Completed	1994	0	Study tour	Know-how transfer	
DE053	LV	Latvian State Institute of Wood Chemistry	Recipient	Bilateral	Obtaining of chemical feedstocks by pyrolysis	Ongoing	0	0	Scientific/research		
DE069	LV	Latvia University of Agriculture	Recipient	Trilateral	Development in forestry and timber industry as well as forest conditions in Latvia since 1985	Completed	1996	0	Scientific/research		
DE073	LV	Latvian Forestry Research Institute Silava	Recipient	Multilateral	EUROPGEN IPGRI Meeting on Hardwoods	Completed	1996	0	Seminar/workshop	Scientific/research	Know-how transfer
DE077	LV	Agriculture University of Latvia	Recipient	Bilateral	Education in forest and timber management and administration	Completed	1996	0	Education/training		
DE104	LV	Agraruniversität Jelgava	Recipient	Bilateral	Training in the forest administration of Brandenburg	Completed	1996	0	Seminar/workshop	Know-how transfer	
DE106	LV	Agraruniversität Jelgava	Recipient	Bilateral	Training in the forest administration of Nordrhein-Westfalen	Completed	1996	0	Seminar/workshop	Know-how transfer	
DE111	LV	University of Jelgava	Recipient	Bilateral	Forest Management - assistance to Latvia	Completed	1997	1997	Education/training		
DE112	LV	University of Jelgava	Recipient	Bilateral	Forestry assistance to Latvia	Completed	1997	1997	Education/training		
DE113	LV	University of Jelgava	Recipient	Bilateral	Forestry assistance to Latvia	Completed	1997	1997	Education/training		
DE114	LV	University of Jelgava	Recipient	Bilateral	Forestry in North Rhine-Westphalia - assistance to Latvia	Completed	1997	1997	Education/training		
DE115	LV	University of Jelgava	Recipient	Bilateral	Agriculture and Forestry in North Rhine-Westphalia - assistance to Latvia	Completed	1997	1997	Education/training		
DE116	LV	University of Jelgava	Recipient	Bilateral	Delivery of teaching materials - assistance to Lativa	Completed	1997	1997	Scientific/research		
DE119	LV	University of Jelgava	Recipient	Bilateral	Introduction in the work of the State Forest Service - assistance to Lativa	Completed	1997	1997	Education/training		
DE120	LV	University of Jelgava	Recipient	Bilateral	Forestry assistance to Lativa	Completed	1998	1998	Education/training		
DE121	LV	University of Jelgava	Recipient	Bilateral	Forest management - assistance to Latvia	Completed	1998	1998	Education/training		
DE122	LV	University of Jelgava	Recipient	Bilateral	Forestry assistance to Latvia	Completed	1998	1998	Education/training		
DE123	LV	University of Jelgava	Recipient	Bilateral	Forestry in North Rhine-Westphalia	Completed	1998	1998	Education/training		
DE124	LV	University of Jelgava	Recipient	Bilateral	Delivery of teaching materials - assistance to Lativa	Completed	1998	1998	Scientific/research		
DE130	LV	University of Jelgava	Recipient	Bilateral	Introduction in the work of the State Forest Service	Completed	1999	1999	Education/training		
DE133	LV	University of Jelgava	Recipient	Bilateral	Forestry in North Rhine-Westphalia	Completed	1999	1999	Education/training		
DE134	LV	University of Jelgava	Recipient	Bilateral	Forestry assistance to Latvia	Completed	1999	1999	Education/training		
DE135	LV	University of Jelgava	Recipient	Bilateral	Forest management - assistance to Latvia	In planning	2000	2000	Education/training		
DE136	LV	University of Jelgava	Recipient	Bilateral	Forestry in North Rhine-Westphalia - assistance to Latvia	In planning	2000	2000	Education/training		

H3 Projects, Recipient Country: *Latvia (continued)*

Project ID		Organization	Position	Cooperation	Title	Status	From/in	To	Type 1	Type 2	Type 3
DK003	LV	Ogre Forestry College and Rural Innovation Centre	Recipient	Bilateral	Introduction of different kinds of education/training within the line of sawmill in Latvia	Completed	1995	1998	Education/training	Know-how transfer	
DK010	LV	Latvian State Forest Service; and Latvian University of Agriculture	Recipient	Bilateral	Supplementary Education in Forest Market Economy for Latvia Forest Graduates in key positions	Completed	1995	1996	Know-how transfer		
DK013	LV		Recipient	Bilateral	Protection of areas for Black Stork and other sensitive species in Latvia's National Forests	Completed	1994				
DK014	LV		Recipient	Bilateral	Introduction and Training of Sustainable Forest Management in the Private Forestry in Latvia and Lithuania.	Completed	1995		Capacity building	Capacity building	
DK015	LV		Recipient	Bilateral	Revision of Latvian Forest Conservation System and Management Plan for Gauja National Park.		1997		Policy/strategy	Capacity building	
DK016	LV		Recipient	Bilateral	Inventories of Spiecies and Habitats, Development of Management Plans and Capacity Bilding in Approximatio...Latvia	In planning	1998	2000	Capacity building	Know-how transfer	
DK045	LV		Recipient	Bilateral	A management plan for Kemiri National Park, Latvia	Ongoing	0	0	Institutional development		
DK046	LV		Recipient	Bilateral	Land consolidation, Gauja National Park in Latvia	Ongoing	0	0	Policy/strategy	National Park Protecti''	
EU001	LV	Min. of Env. Protection and Reg. Development - Env. Protection Dept.	Recipient	Multilateral	Sustainable forestry and forest biodiversity conservation in central-eastern Europe	Completed	1998	2001	Scientific/research	Capacity building	Policy/strategy
FI005	LV		Recipient	Bilateral	Expert seminar on the establishment of a site information system in the Baltic region	Completed	1995	0	Seminar/workshop		
FI011	LV	Ministry of Forestry	Recipient	Bilateral	Development of forest statistics in the Baltic countries (feasibility study)	Completed	1995	0	Scientific/research		
FI015	LV	Latvian Ministry of Agriculture, State Forest Service	Recipient	Bilateral	Development of Forest Owners' and Mechanical Wood Industries' Interest Organisations in Latvia	Completed	1996	1996	Capacity building	Other (study)	
FI016	LV	Latvian Ministry of Agriculture, State Forest Service	Recipient	Bilateral	Seminar on developing the private forest economy in Latvia	Completed	1995	0	Seminar/workshop	Capacity building	
FI018	LV		Recipient	Multilateral	Establishment and start-up of the Baltic Environmental Education Network	Completed	1995	0	Seminar/workshop	Education/training	
FI019	LV	State Forest Service	Recipient	Bilateral	Training project of Certified Graders in Lativa	Completed	1995	1996	Education/training	Know-how transfer	
FI024	LV	State Forest Service	Recipient	Multilateral	Establishment and start-up of the Baltic Environmental Education Network	Completed	1995	0	Seminar/workshop	Education/training	
GB006	LV	State Forest Service	Recipient	Multilateral	Technical Assistance to Ministry of Agriculture Project Management Unit in Latvia	Completed	1995	0	Policy/strategy		
GB016	LV	State Forest Service	Recipient	Bilateral	Support for forestry in Latvia	In planning	1997	0	Study tour	Seminar/workshop	Scientific/research
GB018	LV	State Forest Service	Recipient	Multilateral	Private forestry sector development in Latvia	Completed	1997	0	Study tour	Seminar/workshop	Education/training
GB020	LV	Valsts Mezi	Recipient	Bilateral	Latvia and United Kingdom Forest Certification	Completed	2000	2000	Study tour		
GB022	LV	State Forest Service	Recipient	Bilateral	Forest ecological planning	Ongoing	2000	0	Seminar/workshop	Education/training	

H3 Projects, Recipient Country: *Latvia (continued)*

Project ID		Organization	Position	Cooperation	Title	Status	From/in	To	Type 1	Type 2	Type 3
GB024	LV	WWF, Latvia	Recipient	Bilateral	Field test of Latvian Draft FSC Standard	Completed	1999	1999	Seminar/workshop	Technical development	Know-how transfer
GB026	LV	JSC/ LVM	Recipient	Bilateral	Various consultancy projects in Romania, Slovakia and Latvia on certification of forests.	Completed	2000	0	Seminar/workshop	Technical development	
GB029	LV	Government of Latvia	Recipient	Bilateral	Baltic States Rural Development Project	Ongoing	2000	2003	Know-how transfer		
LT020	LV	Forest Research Institute	Recipient	Bilateral	The Baltic Sawmill industry to the year 2000		1995	1996			
LV001	FA	Food and Agriculture Organization of the United Nations	Donor	Multilateral	Research on grading rules and contract forms to be used in Latvia	Completed			Seminar/workshop	Scientific/research	Capacity building
LV001	LV	State Forest Service	Recipient								
LV002	SE	SIDA	Donor	Bilateral	Forestry inventory using the GIS images	Completed	1995	1996	Education/training	Technical development	Capacity building
LV002	LV	State Forest Service	Recipient								
LV003	LV	Private Forest Owners Assocation	Recipient	Bilateral	Forestry extension	In planning	1996	1997	Seminar/workshop	Education/training	Know-how transfer
LV003	LV	State Forest Service	Recipient								
LV003	SE	SIDA	Donor								
LV004	DK	Ministry of External Affairs	Donor	Bilateral	Forest economy studies in Latvia University of Agriculture	Completed	1995	1996	Seminar/workshop	Education/training	Know-how transfer
LV004	LV	University of Agriculture, Forest Faculty	Recipient								
LV005	SE	SIDA	Donor	Bilateral	Feasibility study for a new green field pulp mill	Completed	1995	1996	Technical development		
LV005	LV	State Forest Service	Recipient								
LV006	DE	BMZ	Donor	Bilateral	Extension/consulting for the private forest industry	Completed	1995	1999	Seminar/workshop	Education/training	
LV006	LV	State Forest Service	Recipient								
LV007	EU	European Community -- Phare	Donor	Multilateral	Technical assistance to the private forestry	In planning	1996	1997	Study tour	Seminar/workshop	Education/training
LV007	LV	State Forest Service	Recipient								
LV007	LV	Association of private forest owners	Recipient								
NO005	LV	DLM	Recipient	Bilateral	Joint venture with Latvia--log cabin production	Completed	0	0	Education/training		
SE005	LV	Ministry of Environmental Protection	Recipient	Bilateral	Nature conservation	Completed	0	0	Study tour	Know-how transfer	
SE009	LV		Recipient	Bilateral	Training course on "Forest management in a market economy"	Completed	1992	0	Education/training		
SE013	LV	Minisy of Forestry	Recipient	Bilateral	Forest policy, legislation and potential cut	Completed	1993	1994	Capacity building		
SE024	LV	Latvia University of Agriculture, Dept. of Wood Processing	Recipient	Bilateral	Training on "Improved quality of sawn wood"	Completed	1996	1996	Education/training		
SE029	LV		Recipient	Bilateral	Key habitat inventories -- a project in Estonia, Latvia, Lithuania.	Ongoing	1999	2004			

H3 Projects, Recipient Country: *Lithuania*

Project ID		Organization	Position	Cooperation	Title	Status	From/in	To	Type 1	Type 2	Type 3
DE026	LT	College of Forestry, Kaunas	Recipient	Bilateral	Education of three students from Lithuania at the College of Forestry	Completed	1995	0	Education/training		

H3 Projects, Recipient Country: *Lithuania (continued)*

Project ID		Organization	Position	Cooperation	Title	Status	From/in	To	Type 1	Type 2	Type 3
DE034	LT	State Forest Service	Recipient	Bilateral	Support of Lithuanian Forest Service	Completed	1994	1995	Study tour		
DE058	LT	Lithuanian Forest Research Institute	Recipient	Bilateral	Biomarkers in coniferous trees	Completed	1995	1998	Scientific/research		
DE073	LT	Lithuanian Forest Research Institute	Recipient	Multilateral	EUROPGEN IPGRI Meeting on Hardwoods	Completed	1996	0	Seminar/workshop	Scientific/research	Know-how transfer
DE097	LT	Lithuanian Forest Ministry	Recipient	Bilateral	Visit of 4 Lithuanian forest experts	Completed	1994	1996	Seminar/workshop	Education/training	Know-how transfer
DE102	LT	Ministry of Agriculture of Lithuania	Recipient	Bilateral	Post graduate study	Completed	1995	1998	Education/training		
DE103	LT	Akademija	Recipient	Bilateral	Study of the situation in the forestry of Lithuania especially in fulture and stand treatment	Completed	1996	0	Scientific/research		
DE126	LT	Ministry of Agriculture	Recipient	Bilateral	Exchange of experience in forestry	Completed	1998	1998	Study tour		
DE131	LT	Ministry of Agriculture	Recipient	Bilateral	Exchange of experience in forestry	Completed	1999	1999	Study tour		
DE132	LT	Ministry of Env., Dept. of Forestry	Recipient	Bilateral	Studies in forestry	Ongoing	1998	2001	Education/training		
DK004	LT		Recipient	Multilateral	Introduction of different kinds of education/training within the line of sawmill in Latvia		0	0	Education/training		
DK006	LT	Kaunas Higher School of Forestry	Recipient	Bilateral	Forestry training and education in Lithuania	In planning	1996	1997	Seminar/workshop	Education/training	
DK007	LT	Vilnius State Forest District	Recipient	Bilateral	Sustainable development and use of forest resources in Lithuania	In planning	0	0	Education/training	Technical development	Capacity building
DK007	LT	Kaunas Forest Faculty	Recipient	Bilateral	Sustainable development and use of forest resources in Lithuania	In planning	0	0	Education/training	Technical development	Capacity building
DK007	LT	Agricultural Advisory Center	Recipient	Bilateral	Sustainable development and use of forest resources in Lithuania	In planning	0	0	Education/training	Technical development	Capacity building
DK014	LT		Recipient	Bilateral	Introduction and Training of Sustainable Forest Management in the Private Forestry in Latvia and Lithuania.	Completed	1995		Capacity building		
DK018	LT		Recipient	Bilateral	Multiple-Use Forest Management Planing in Lithuania	Completed	1995	0	Education/training		
DK020	LT		Recipient	Bilateral	Integrated Control Programme for Lymantria monacha in Lithuanian Forest for 1996	Completed	1996	0			
DK022	LT		Recipient	Bilateral	State Park Institutional Development Project, Lithuania	Completed	1998	1999	Education/training	Capacity building	Know-how transfer
DK032	LT		Recipient	Bilateral	Integrating environmental values into Lithuanian Forestry	Completed	1996	1996''			
DK036	LT		Recipient	Bilateral	Sustainable forest management for Lithuanian forest owners on institutional and capacity building in their organisations and the advisory service	Completed	0	0	Capacity building	Institutional development	
EU001	LT	Min. of Env. Protection - Landscape & Biodiversity Dept.	Recipient	Multilateral	Sustainable forestry and forest biodiversity conservation in central-eastern Europe	Completed	1998	2001	Scientific/research	Capacity building	Policy/strategy
FA005	LT	Government of Lithuania	Recipient	Multilateral	Control of nun moth and pine caterpillars.	Completed	1995	0	Education/training	Technical development	Know-how transfer

H3 Projects, Recipient Country: *Lithuania (continued)*

Project ID		Organization	Position	Cooperation	Title	Status	From/in	To	Type 1	Type 2	Type 3
FI005	LT		Recipient	Bilateral	Expert seminar on the establishment of a site information system in the Baltic region	Completed	1995	0	Seminar/workshop		
FI011	LT	Ministry of Forestry	Recipient	Bilateral	Development of forest statistics in the Baltic countries (feasibility study)	Completed	1995	0	Scientific/research		
FI014	LT	Lithuanian Agricultural Academy	Recipient	Bilateral	Education of Baltic experts, adaptation of the Finnish MELA-system for forestry analysis in Baltic countries	Completed	1995	1996	Scientific/research	Capacity building	Know-how transfer
FI018	LT		Recipient	Multilateral	Establishment and start-up of the Baltic Environmental Education Network	Completed	1995	0	Seminar/workshop	Education/training	
FI021	LT	Ministry of Forestry	Recipient	Bilateral	Preparation of Project Document for forestry development in Birzai Forest Enterprise	Completed	1994	1995	Capacity building		
FI021	LT	Birzai Forest Enterprise	Recipient	Bilateral	Preparation of Project Document for forestry development in Birzai Forest Enterprise	Completed	1994	1995	Capacity building		
FI022	LT	Ministry of Forestry	Recipient	Bilateral	Forest development strategy and implementation under the market economy conditions in Birzai Forest Enterprise *	Completed	1995	1997	Capacity building	Know-how transfer	
FI022	LT	Birzai Forest Enterprise	Recipient	Bilateral	Forest development strategy and implementation under the market economy conditions in Birzai Forest Enterprise *	Completed	1995	1997	Capacity building	Know-how transfer	
FI024	LT		Recipient	Multilateral	Establishment and start-up of the Baltic Environmental Education Network	Completed	1995	0	Seminar/workshop	Education/training	
GB001	LT	Dzukija National Park	Recipient	Bilateral	To evaluate Technical Assistance for Ozukija National Park	Ongoing	0	0	Policy/strategy		
GB029	LT		Recipient	Bilateral	Baltic States Rural Development Project	Ongoing	2000	2003	Know-how transfer		
IE003	LT	Ministry of Environmental Protection	Recipient	Multilateral	Assistance in the development of a national environmental strategy and action programme for Lithuania	Completed	0	0	Policy/strategy		
LT001	DK	Hedeselskabet	Donor	Bilateral	Multiple use of forest in Dubrava experimental Forest Enterprise	Completed	1995	1996	Know-how transfer		
LT001	LT	Ministry of Forestry	Recipient								
LT002	SE	Jaakko Poyry AB	Donor	Bilateral	Forest Sector Development Plan (FSDP)	Completed	1993	1998	Know-how transfer		
LT002	LT	Ministry of Forestry	Recipient								
LT003	NO	Ministry of Forestry	Donor	Multilateral	Modernisation of Nursery of Dubrava Experimental Forest Enterprise	Completed	1996	1997	Technical development	Know-how transfer	
LT003	LT	Ministry of Forestry	Recipient								
LT003	EU	European Community -- Phare	Donor								
LT004	DK	Danish Ministry of Env. and Energy	Donor	Bilateral	Multiple use of Forest in Dubrava Experimental Forest Enterprise	Completed	1995	1996			
LT004	LT	Min.of Forestry/Environmental Protection, Forest Mgmt.Inst, Dubrava Exp. Forest Ent.	Recipient								
LT005	EU	Phare	Donor	Bilateral	Dubrava nursery modernization project	Completed	1996	1997	Education/training		
LT005	LT	Ministry of Forestry	Recipient								

H3 Projects, Recipient Country: Lithuania (continued)

Project ID		Organization	Position	Cooperation	Title	Status	From/in	To	Type 1	Type 2	Type 3
LT006	FI	Finish Ministry of Agriculture and Forestry/Nordic Council of Ministers	Donor	Bilateral	Development of forest statistics in the Baltic and Nordic States	Completed	1996	1997	Scientific/research	Other, (conference)	
LT006	LT	Ministry of Agriculture and Forestry of Lithuania and Centre of Forest Economics	Recipient								
LT007	DK	Danish Ministry of Env. and Energy	Donor	Bilateral	State Park Institutional Development Project	Completed	1997	2000	Policy/strategy		
LT007	LT	Ministry of Environmen	Recipient								
LT008	LT		Recipient	Bilateral	Training in business companies - Advertising of research, running small rural business companies		0	0	Education/training		
LT008	GB	Wales University	Donor								
LT009	LT	Kaunas Technological University	Recipient	Multilateral	Measurement and grading of pulpwood		1997	0	Education/training		
LT009	SE	JAKKO POYRY Consulting AB	Recipient								
LT010	LT	Min. of Environment Protection and Ministry of Forestry of Lithuania	Recipient	Multilateral	International cooperative programme on assessment and monitoring of air pollution effects on forest. Level-1		1988	0	Scientific/research		
LT011	LT	Min. of Environment Protection and Min. of Forestry of Lithuania	Recipient	Multilateral	International cooperative programme on the intensive monitoring of forest ecosystems		1995	0	Scientific/research		
LT012	LT	Min. of Environment and Min. of Forestry of Lithuania	Recipient	Multilateral	International cooperative programme on assessment and monitoring of air pollution effects on forest, and forest soil condition		1995	0	Scientific/research		
LT013	LT	Min. of Agriculture and Forestry	Donor	Multilateral	"EUFORGEN"--European forest genetic resources		1995	1997	Scientific/research		
LT014	LT	Forest Research Institute and other 7 institutions from Lithuania	Recipient	Bilateral	Conservation of plant genetic resources in the Baltic States		1994	1997	Scientific/research		
LT015	LT	Forest Research Institute	Recipient	Bilateral	Crown transparency and radial growth of trees		1995	1997	Scientific/research		
LT015	DE		Donor								
LT016	LT	Forest Research Institute	Recipient	Bilateral	Biomarkers in coniferous trees		1995	1998	Scientific/research		
LT016	DE		Donor								
LT017	SE	JAAKKO POYRY Consulting AB	Donor	Bilateral	Lithuanian forest sector development program. Project 2. National monitoring and management information		1996	0	Scientific/research		
LT017	LT	Forest Research Institute	Recipient								
LT018	SE	Dept. of Forest Mycology and pathology of Forest Genetics, Univ. of Agri. Sciences	Donor	Bilateral	Joint studies on forest pathology		1994	1997	Scientific/research		
LT018	LT	Forest Research Institute	Recipient								

H3 Projects, Recipient Country: *Lithuania (continued)*

Project ID		Organization	Position	Cooperation	Title	Status	From/in	To	Type 1	Type 2	Type 3
LT019	LT	Forest Research Institute	Recipient	Bilateral	Joint studies on forest genetics (3 projects)		1995	1997	Scientific/research		
LT019	SE	Dept. of Forest Genetics of Swedish University of Agricultural Sciences	Donor								
LT020	FI	Dept. of Forest Economics, Helsinki University	Donor	Bilateral	The Baltic Sawmill industry to the year 2000		1995	1996			
LT020	LV	Forest Research Institute	Recipient								
LT021					Introduction of the concept sustainable forest management in the private forestry in Latvia and Lithuania		1995	1997	Education/training		
LT021	DK		Donor	Bilateral							
LT021	LT	Forest Research Institute	Recipient								
LT022	LT	Forest Research Institute	Recipient	Multilateral	International symposium on "Insitu conservation of plant genetic diversity"	Completed	1996	0	Scientific/research		
LT023	LT	Forest Research Institute	Recipient	Multilateral	"Nordic Group Meeting" - Annual meeting on forest genetics and tree breeding.		1996	0	Scientific/research		
LT024	LT	Forest Research Institute	Recipient	Bilateral	Conference on "Conservation of genetic resources in natural forestry: management and environment protection".		0	0	Scientific/research	Conference	
LT024	DE	Institute for Forest Tree Breeding, Weldsieversdorf	Donor								
LT025	SE	Dept. of Forest genetics of Swedish University of Agricultural Sciences	Donor	Bilateral	Long-term studies (scholarships) on forest genetics		1995	1997	Education/training		
LT025	LT	Lithuanian Forest Research Institute	Recipient								
LT026	LT	Forest Research Institute	Recipient	Bilateral	Long-term studies (scholarships) on forest pathology		1995	1997	Education/training		
LT026	SE	Dept. of Forest Mycology and Pathology of Swedish Univ. of Agri. Sciences	Donor								
LT027	SE		Donor	Bilateral	Technical training course on database management of INTRANET and INTERNET		0	0	Education/training		
LT027	LT	Forest Research Institute	Recipient								
LT028	LT	Forest Research Institute	Recipient	Bilateral	Long-term technical training in nursery production		0	0	Education/training	Technical assistance	
LT028	EU	Phare PROJECT	Donor								
LT029	DK	Association of Danish Forest Owner Cooperations	Donor	Bilateral	Courses on "Introduction of the concept sustainable forest management in the private forestry in Latvia and Lithuania		1996	0	Education/training		
LT029	LT	Forest Research Institute	Recipient								
LT030	NO	Vinterlandbruksskolen	Donor	Bilateral	Motormanual silviculture aimed at private forest owners		1996	0	Education/training		
LT030	LT	Kaunas Forestry College, Forest owners' assocation	Recipient								

H3 Projects, Recipient Country: Lithuania (continued)

Project ID		Organization	Position	Cooperation	Title	Status	From/in	To	Type 1	Type 2	Type 3
LT031	LT	Kaunas Forestry College	Recipient	Multilateral	Professional training of sawmill workers		1996	0	Education/training		
LT031	EU	EU/Phare	Donor								
LT032	SE	BITS, Naturbruks Gymnasiet	Donor	Bilateral	Development of Forest Vocational training in Lithuania		1995	1997	Education/training		
LT032	LT	Kaunas Forest.y College/Arkliskes Agri. School	Recipient								
LT033	LT	Lithuania Forest Owners Association	Recipient	Bilateral	Join meeting to elaborate projects.		1997	0	Education/training		
LT033	SE	Swedish Forest Owners Confederation	Donor								
LT034	SE	Swedish Forest Owners Confederation	Donor	Bilateral	Visit to Swedish Forest Owners Confederation and Associations		1996	0	Education/training		
LT034	LT	Lithuania Forest Owners Association	Recipient								
LT035	LT	Forest Research Institute	Recipient	Bilateral	Multiple use of forest in Dubrava Experimental Forest Enterprise	Completed	1997	0	Education/training		
LT035	LT	University of Agriculture, Lithuania	Recipient								
LT035	LT	Forest Economy Centre	Recipient								
LT035	LT	Institute of Forest Management and Inventory	Recipient								
LT035	DK	Danish Ministry of Env. and Energy	Donor								
LT036	RU		Donor	Multilateral	International meeting of specialists on forest inventory and management		1997	0	Education/training		
LT036	LT		Recipient								
LT037	SE	SIDA and Jakko Poyry	Donor	Bilateral	Pilot study project for implementation of national forest inventory by sampling methods in Lithuanian forests.		1996	1997	Technical development	Scientific/research	
LT037	LT	Forestry Dept, Institute of Forest Management and Inventory	Recipient								
LT038	SE	SIDA, and Jakko Poyry	Donor	Bilateral	Created methodical and theoretical base for forest dynamic forecasting model		1996	1997	Technical development	Scientific/research	
LT038	LT	Forestry Dept, Institute of Forest Management and Inventory	Recipient								
LT039	SE	SIDA, and Jakko Poyry	Donor	Bilateral	Two seminars/workshops on the national forest inventory and forest dynamic modelling		1996	1997	Seminar/workshop		
LT039	LT	Forestry Dept, Institute of Forest Management and Inventory	Recipient								
LT040	DK	WWF	Donor	Bilateral	Management plans and programmes for Nemunas River Delta Regional Park, Luthuania	Completed	1996	1999	Study tour	Seminar/workshop	Scientific/research

H3 Projects, Recipient Country: *Lithuania (continued)*

Project ID		Organization	Position	Cooperation	Title	Status	From/in	To	Type 1	Type 2	Type 3
LT040	LT	Dept. of Forest and Projected Areas	Recipient								
LT041	FA	Food and Agriculture Organization of the United Nations	Donor	Bilateral	Development of the private forestry sector in Lithuania	Completed	1998	2000	Seminar/workshop	Scientific/research	Technical development
LT041	LT	Dept. of Forests and Protected areas	Recipient								
LT042	SE	Swedish National Energy Administration	Donor	Bilateral	Wood fuel development in Lithuania Phase I	Completed	2000	2000	Know-how transfer		
LT042	LT	Dept. of Forests and Protected Areas, Ministry of Environment	Recipient								
LT043	LT	Dept. of Forests and Protected Areas	Recipient	Bilateral	Afforestation of abandoned agricultural land based on sustainable planing and environmentally sound forest management.	Ongoing	1999	2001	Study tour	Scientific/research	Technical development
LT043	DK	Danish Environment Protection Agency	Donor								
LT044	SE		Donor	Bilateral	Pilot Woodland Key Habitat Inventory in Lithuania	Ongoing	2001	2002	Technical assistance		
LT044	LT		Recipient								
LT045	LT		Recipient	Bilateral	Wood Fuel Development in Lithuania, Phase II	Ongoing	2001	2002	Know-how transfer		
LT045	SE		Donor								
NO006	LT	UAB dominga	Recipient	Bilateral	Training and production of solid oak boards for furniture production	Completed	0	0	Education/training		
PL006	LT	Lietuvos Misku Instituta	Recipient	Multilateral	Lymantriamonacha (nun moth) control treatment	Suggested	1996	1997	Scientific/research		
SE006	LT	Ministry of Forestry of the Republic of Lithuania	Recipient	Bilateral	Improving of quality of sawnwood	Completed	1995	0	Seminar/workshop	Capacity building	
SE008	LT	Kaunas forestry College	Recipient	Bilateral	Development of forest vocational training in Lithuania	Completed	1995	1996	Education/training		
SE011	LT		Recipient	Bilateral	Training course on "Forest management in a market economy"	Completed	1993	0	Education/training		
SE014	LT		Recipient	Bilateral	Forestry Sector Master Plan	Completed	1993	0	Policy/strategy		
SE015	LT		Recipient	Bilateral	1-week Seminar on "Use of domestic fuel"	Completed	1994	0	Seminar/workshop		
SE017	LT		Recipient	Bilateral	Research project on "Forests along watercourses"	Completed	1994	0	Scientific/research		
SE029	LT		Recipient	Bilateral	Key habitat inventories -- a project in Estonia, Latvia, Lithuania.	Ongoing	1999	2004			
SE030	LT		Recipient	Bilateral	Wood fuel development -- a project in Lithuania, Russian Federation	Ongoing	2000	2004			

H3 Projects, Recipient Country: *Poland*

Project ID		Organization	Position	Cooperation	Title	Status	From/in	To	Type 1	Type 2	Type 3
AT019	PL	SGGW Warszawa	Recipient	Multilateral	Computer-aided teaching of forest economics	Completed	1991	1994	Technical development	Education/training	Other: Tempus Jep
AT027	PL	Lasy Panstwowe	Recipient	Bilateral	Forest management in mountainous areas	Completed	1995	1996	Study tour		
AT030	PL	Forest Research Institute Warszawa	Recipient	Multilateral	Marketing of Forest Enterprises	Completed	1994	0	Seminar/workshop		

H3 Projects, Recipient Country: *Poland (continued)*

Project ID		Organization	Position	Cooperation	Title	Status	From/in	To	Type 1	Type 2	Type 3
AT031	PL		Recipient	Bilateral	Study Tour--Forestry in mountainous areas	Completed	1995	0	Study tour	Know-how transfer	Know-how transfer
AT032	PL		Recipient	Bilateral	Study Tour--Forestry in mountainous areas	Completed	1995	0	Study tour		
AT038	PL		Recipient	Bilateral	Study Tour--Forest management	Completed	1995	0	Study tour		
AT046	PL		Recipient	Bilateral	Study tour on Management of protection of forests	Completed	1997	0	Study tour		
CZ025	PL	Polish Academy of Sciences, Institute of Botany	Recipient	Multilateral	Evaluation of ozone air pollution and its phytotoxic potential in the Carpathian forests	Completed	1997	0	Scientific/research		
CZ026	PL	Forest Research Institute	Recipient	Multilateral	Scenario analysis of sustainable wood production under different forest management regimes (SCEFORMA)	Ongoing	1998	2001	Scientific/research		
DE003	PL	Zespol Ochrony Lasu	Donor	Trilateral	"Black Triangle" Schwarzes Dreieck--Specific working group forest protection and hunting	Completed	1993	0	Study tour	Policy/strategy	Know-how transfer
DE010	PL	Geobot. Stat. Bialow.	Donor	Bilateral	Comparison of virgin and managed forest stands/Bialowieza/E-Poland	Completed	0	0	Study tour	Scientific/research	
DE024	PL	Akademia Rolnicza	Recipient	Bilateral	Training in practice of vitro culture	Completed	1994	0	Education/training		
DE044	PL	Staat. Forstl. Forschungsinst.	Recipient	Bilateral	Market analysis for untreated wood and wood products in Poland and of the Polish foreign trade with Germany	In planning	1996	1999	Scientific/research		
DE048	PL	RDLP	Recipient	Bilateral	Exchange of informations and experiences on special field of forestry work	Completed	1992	0	Education/training	Know-how transfer	
DE048	PL	RDLP	Donor	Bilateral	Exchange of informations and experiences on special field of forestry work	Completed	1992	0	Education/training	Know-how transfer	
DE051	PL	University	Recipient	Bilateral	Dendrochronology	Completed	1995	0	Scientific/research	Know-how transfer	
DE063	PL	Univ. of Agriculture, Dept. of Silviculture	Recipient	Multilateral	Joint workshops BRNO-THARANDT	Ongoing	0	0	Seminar/workshop	Seminar/workshop	
DE068	PL	Agricultural University of Poznan, Faculty of Wood Technology	Recipient	Bilateral	Production and marketing of Polish particle boards solid timber boards--standards in Poland and Germany in the area	Completed	1995	0	Scientific/research		
DE072	PL	Geobot. Stat. Bialow.	Donor	Bilateral	Comparison of virgin and managed forest stands/Bialowieza/E-Poland	Ongoing	0	0	Study tour	Scientific/research	
DE086	PL	Forest Administration, Wojewodschaft	Recipient	Bilateral	Exchange of information, harmonize activities on forest problems	Completed	1996	0	Policy/strategy		
DE098	PL	Ministry of Environment Protech, Natural Resources and Forestry	Recipient	Bilateral	Special seminar for forest experts	Completed	1995	0	Seminar/workshop	Know-how transfer	Know-how transfer
DE110	PL	Akademie Rolnicza, Wydzial Lesny	Recipient	Bilateral	Exchange of experience with forest faculty of Akademie Rolnicza and Krakau - assistance to Poland	Completed	1996	0	Study tour	Scientific/research	Know-how transfer
DE118	PL	Administration of Corzow and Szczecin	Recipient	Bilateral	Introduction in the work of the State Forest Service - assistance to Poland.	Completed	1997	1997	Education/training	"	"
DK001	PL	Zespol Szkol Lesnych	Recipient	Bilateral	Training of Polich forest workers	Completed	1993	1995	Education/training	Capacity building	Know-how transfer
DK005	PL	Polish Forestry Department	Donor	Bilateral	Implementation of the policy of the sustainable forestry development in Poland	Completed	0	0	Seminar/workshop		
DK005	PL		Recipient	Bilateral	Implementation of the policy of the sustainable forestry development in Poland	Completed	0	0	Seminar/workshop		

H3 Projects, Recipient Country: *Poland (continued)*

Project ID		Organization	Position	Cooperation	Title	Status	From/in	To	Type 1	Type 2	Type 3
DK023	PL		Recipient	Bilateral	Transfer of Know-how to the Project of Utilization of Wood Chips in Poland	Completed	1992	1993	Know-how transfer		
DK024	PL		Recipient	Bilateral	Integrated Control Programme for Lymantria monacha in Polish Forest	Completed	1994	0	Know-how transfer	Financial assistance	
DK025	PL		Recipient	Bilateral	Sustainable Afforestation on the Marginally Productive Lands at Baltic Costal Lowlands of Poland	Completed	1997	0	Know-how transfer		
DK026	PL		Recipient	Bilateral	Introducing Multiple-Use Principles into Forest Management in the Superintendency Kliniska, Poland	Completed	1997	0	Know-how transfer		
DK037	PL		Recipient	Bilateral	Development of centre for nature and forestry education in Rogon.	Ongoing	0	0	Capacity building	Institutional development	Education/training
DK043	PL		Recipient	Bilateral	Sustainable production and use of wood residues for energy purposes, Wejherowo, Gdansk Region, Poland	Ongoing	0	0	Technical assistance	''	''
EF001	PL		Recipient	Multilateral	Growth Trend of European Forests	Completed	1996	0	Scientific/research		
EP001	PL	Ministry of Environmental Protection	Recipient	Multilateral	Support to policy and guidelines for sustainable management of temperate forest ecosystems *	Completed	1994	1995	Policy/strategy		
EU001	PL	Dept. of State Forestry, Min. of Env. Protect., Natural Res. & Forestry	Recipient	Multilateral	Sustainable forestry and forest biodiversity conservation in central-eastern Europe	Completed	1998	2001	Scientific/research	Capacity building	Policy/strategy
FO002	PL	Polish Academy of Science	Recipient	Multilateral	IUFRO/SPDC Travel Grants	Completed	1994	0	Other(Travel grant)		
FO002	PL	Agricultural University of Poznan	Recipient	Multilateral	IUFRO/SPDC Travel Grants	Completed	1994	0	Other(Travel grant)		
FO003	PL	Forest Research Institute	Recipient	Multilateral	IUFRO/SPDC travel grants	Completed	1994	0	Other (travel grant)		
FR004	PL	PAN-J-DENDROL	Recipient	Trilateral	Technical and scientific cooperation in forestry research	Completed	1994	1997	Scientific/research		
FR005	PL	INRA	Recipient	Bilateral	Technical and scientific cooperation in forestry research	Suggested	1996	1999	Scientific/research		
FR006	PL	Institut de Dendrologie	Recipient	Bilateral	Technical and scientific cooperation in forestry research	Suggested	1996	0	Scientific/research		
FR007	PL	INRA	Recipient	Bilateral	Technical and scientific cooperation in forestry research	Suggested	1996	1999	Scientific/research		
FR008	PL	INRA	Recipient	Bilateral	Technical and scientific cooperation in forestry research	Suggested	1996	1999	Scientific/research		
GB002	PL	General Directorate of State Forests	Recipient	Multilateral	Polish Forest Development Programme	Completed	1995	0	Study tour		
GB003	PL	National Fund for Environmental Protection	Recipient	Multilateral	Forestry Development Programme 1994	Completed	1994	0	Technical development		
GB008	PL	General Directorate of State Forests	Recipient	Bilateral	Visit by General Directorate of State Forests in Poland	Completed	1995	1995	Study tour		
GB014	PL	Gdansk City Council	Recipient	Bilateral	Management of natural resources Phase I.	Completed	1994	1997	Technical development		
GB027	PL	Various institutions listed for data etc.	Recipient	Multilateral	PhD Scholarship (Wiliam M. Barrelt)	Completed	2000	0	Scientific/research		

H3 Projects, Recipient Country: *Poland (continued)*

Project ID		Organization	Position	Cooperation	Title	Status	From/in	To	Type 1	Type 2	Type 3
GB036	PL		Recipient	Bilateral	Training on specific topics for a group of 4/5 NGOs including Agenda 21 and permaculture.	Completed	2000	0	Education/training		
IE002	PL	National Fund for Environmental Protection and Water Management	Recipient	Multilateral	Technical assistance for programme management for the Forestry Development Programme	Completed	1995	0	Technical development		
IT003	PL	Government of Poland	Recipient	Bilateral	Agreement Italy-Poland for the conversion of the debts into Environmental Protection initiatives (Ekofundus).	Ongoing	1998	2009	Financial assistance		
NO016	PL	Koscierzyna,	Recipient	Bilateral	Koscierzyna; Development of wood product factory	Completed	1997	0	Technical development		
PL001	EU	Phare programme, European Commission	Donor	Multilateral	Forestry Development Programme	Completed	1995	1997	Scientific/research	Technical development	Know-how transfer
PL001	PL	General Directorate of State Forests	Recipient								
PL002	PL	MEPNRF	Recipient	Multilateral	Instructions for nature conservation programme	Ongoing	0	0	Seminar/workshop		
PL002	EP	UNEP, Regional Office for Europe	Donor								
PL003	DE	Bundesministrium für ernahrung Landwirschaft und forsten	Donor	Bilateral	The State supervision of private forests	Ongoing	0	0	Study tour	Seminar/workshop	
PL003	PL	MOS, ZNIL	Recipient								
PL004	PL	Forest Research Institute	Recipient	Multilateral	Ecological and economic evaluation of the impact of nun moth control treatments on the forest environment	Ongoing	0	0	Seminar/workshop	Education/training	Scientific/research
PL004	EU	Phare Programme	Donor								
PL005	PL	Forest Research Institute	Recipient	Bilateral	Integrated control of lymantria monacha in Polish forest and economical impact studies.	Ongoing	0	0	Seminar/workshop	Scientific/research	
PL005	DK	DEPA/Royal Vet. and A. University	Donor								
PL006	DK	Depa/Royal Veterinary and A. University	Donor	Multilateral	Lymantriamonacha (nun moth) control treatment	Suggested	1996	1997	Scientific/research	Capacity building	
PL006	PL	Forest Research Institute	Recipient								
PL006	BY	Forest Institute of Bas	Recipient								
PL006	LT	Lietuvos Misku Instituta	Recipient								
PL007	IB	European Investment Bank, Luxembourg	Donor	Multilateral	Development of selected forestry branches and protection of ecosystems in National Parks in 1993-1997	Completed	1993	1997	Education/training	Technical development	Policy/strategy
PL007	PL	Ministry of Environment Natural Resources and Forestry	Recipient								
PL007	WB	The World Bank	Donor								
PL007	DK	Ministry of Agriculture, The Danish School of Forestry	Donor								
PL007	SE	SIDA	Donor								

H3 Projects, Recipient Country: *Poland (continued)*

Project ID		Organization	Position	Cooperation	Title	Status	From/in	To	Type 1	Type 2	Type 3
PL007	PL	General Directorate of State Forests	Recipient								
PL008	WB	World Bank, Global Env. Facility	Donor	Bilateral	Forest biodiversity protection project	Completed	1992	1995	Seminar/workshop	Education/training	Scientific/research
PL008	PL	Ministry of Env. Prot., Natural Resources and Forestry	Recipient								
PL009	EU	European Community	Donor	Multilateral	Genetic diversity of forest tree species in central Europe	Suggested	1996	1998	Scientific/research		
PL009	PL	Forest Research Institute	Recipient								
PL009	BY	Byelarussin Academy of Science, Forest Institute	Recipient								
PL009	AT	Forest Research Centre	Recipient								
PL010	SE	Swedish Board for Investment and Technical Support	Donor	Bilateral	Use of GIS and Satellite Remote Sensing for ..... of afforestation at regional and local level	Completed	1995	1996	Education/training	Scientific/research	Know-how transfer
PL010	PL	Forestry Research Institute	Recipient								
PL011	NL	DLO Winand Staring Centre (SC-DLO)	Donor	Multilateral	Impacts of climatic change on soil organic matter in lowland forests counter-acted by regeneration management *	Suggested	1996	2000	Study tour	Seminar/workshop	Education/training
PL011	PL	Forest Research Institute, Natural Forest Dept.	Recipient								
PL011	NL	DLO Institute for Forestry & Nature Research (IBN-DLO)	Donor								
PL011	GB	The Forestry Authority Research Division	Donor								
SE025	PL	General Directorate of State Forests	Recipient	Bilateral	Seminar on Polish-Swedish forestry	Completed	1997	1997	Seminar/workshop		
UA005	PL		Donor	Multilateral	Effects of Air Pollution on Forests Health and Biodiversity in forests of the Carpathian Mountains (Programme of IUFRO-SPDC)	Completed	1997	2001	Scientific/research		
UA009	PL		Donor	Multilateral	Scenario analysis of sustainable wood production under different forest management regimes (SCEFORMA) (INCO-Copernicus programme)	Ongoing	1998	2001	Education/training	Technical assistance	
UA011	PL		Donor	Multilateral	Scientific background of reforestation and afforestation improvement activities in Carpathian mountains	Ongoing	2000	0	Scientific/research		

H3 Projects, Recipient Country: *Romania*

Project ID		Organization	Position	Cooperation	Title	Status	From/in	To	Type 1	Type 2	Type 3
AT008	RO	Forest Research and Management Institute	Recipient	Bilateral	Training--Phytopathology	Completed	1994	0	Education/training		
DE025	RO	Suceava, Fac. Forestičre	Recipient	Multilateral	Promotion of education in the field of environmental protection (TEMPUS)	Completed	1994	1997	Education/training	Policy/strategy	Know-how transfer

H3 Projects, Recipient Country: *Romania (continued)*

Project ID		Organization	Position	Cooperation	Title	Status	From/in	To	Type 1	Type 2	Type 3
DE049	RO	Institute Biological Research	Recipient	Bilateral	Analysis of land use patterns in Scarisoara/Romania	In planning	1996	0	Scientific/research		
DE051	RO	University	Recipient	Bilateral	Dendrochronology	Completed	1995	0	Scientific/research	Know-how transfer	
DE100	RO	University Suceava, Forestry Faculty	Recipient	Multilateral	Development of forestry education as a profession for the protection of environment	Ongoing	0	0	Seminar/workshop	Education/training	Capacity building
DK033	RO		Recipient	Bilateral	Sustainable Management and Biological Conservation of the Ceahlau Nature Reserve in Romania	Completed	1997	1997	Know-how transfer		
EU001	RO	Min. of Waters, Forests and Envir. Protection	Recipient	Multilateral	Sustainable forestry and forest biodiversity conservation in central-eastern Europe	Completed	1998	2001	Scientific/research	Capacity building	Policy/strategy
FO004	RO	Forest Research and Management Institute	Recipient	Multilateral	IUFRO/SPDC travel grants	Completed	1994	0	Other (travel grant)		
FO009	RO	Transylvania University Faculty of Silviculture & Forest Eng.	Recipient	Multilateral	IUFRO/SPDC travel grants	Completed	1995	0	Other (travel grants)		
FR009	RO	ASAS	Recipient	Bilateral	Technical and scientific cooperation in forestry research	Suggested	1996	2001	Scientific/research		
FR010	RO		Recipient	Trilateral	Technical and scientific cooperation in forestry research	Completed	1990	1996	Scientific/research		
FR014	RO	INL	Recipient	Trilateral	Creation of a Vocational Training Centre of advanced wood processing techniques in Romania	In planning	1997	0	Technical development		
GB026	RO	WWF (funded by World Bank)	Recipient	Bilateral	Various consultancy projects in Romania, Slovakia and Latvia on certification of forests.	Completed	2000	0	Seminar/workshop	Technical development	Know-how transfer
GB030	RO		Recipient	Bilateral	Project aimed at raisinge public profiles of environmental NGOs and at improving their information programmes	Completed	1999	0	Policy/strategy		
IE006	RO	University of Erasov	Recipient	Trilateral	Brazov University Forestry Project	Completed	1994	0	Education/training		
RO001	RO		Donor		Genetic resources of broad-leaved forest tree species in southern Europe	Ongoing	1997	2003	Other, forest monitoring		
UA005	RO		Donor	Multilateral	Effects of Air Pollution on Forests Health and Biodiversity in forests of the Carpathian Mountains (Programme of IUFRO-SPDC)	Completed	1997	2001	Scientific/research		
UA011	RO		Donor	Multilateral	Scientific background of reforestation and afforestation improvement activities in Carpathian mountains	Ongoing	2000	0	Scientific/research		

H3 Projects, Recipient Country: *Russia*

Project ID		Organization	Position	Cooperation	Title	Status	From/in	To	Type 1	Type 2	Type 3
AT010	RU	Forsttechnische Akademie	Recipient	Bilateral	Simulation model of the forest sector for a region with strong impacts of human activities	Completed	1996	1997	Scientific/research		
AT015	RU	Institute for Biological Problems of the North Russian Academy of Science (IBPN)	Recipient	Bilateral	Comparative studies in endemic East-Siberian grouse species: case study Sibirian spruce grouse	Completed	1995	1997	Scientific/research	Know-how transfer	Policy/strategy
CH002	RU		Recipient	Bilateral	The Pechoro-Ilych Model Project	Completed	1995	1999	Education/training	Technical development	Capacity building
CH002	RU	State Forest Service	Recipient								

H3 Projects, Recipient Country: Russia (continued)

Project ID		Organization	Position	Cooperation	Title	Status	From/in	To	Type 1	Type 2	Type 3
CH002	RU	Ministry of Environment	Recipient								
CH002	RU	Academy of Sciences	Recipient								
DE012	RU	Perner Gebietskomitee für Umweltschutz	Recipient	Bilateral	Cooperation of forestry in the Region Perm	Completed	1994	0	Technical development	Know-how transfer	
DE015	RU	Russian Academy of Sciences	Donor	Bilateral	Ecological-genetic effects of anthropogenous influences on forest ecosystems	Completed	1995	0	Scientific/research		
DE015	RU	Russian Academy of Sciences	Donor								
DE016	RU	Institute for Wood Biology	Recipient	Bilateral	Anatomical and fine-structural investigations of wood	Completed	1995	0	Scientific/research		
DE016	RU	Laboratory Ecol. Monitoring	Recipient								
DE019	RU	Forsttechnische Akademie, St. Petersburg	Recipient	Bilateral	Study tour in the new federal states/standards for environment	Completed	1995	1996	Study tour		
DE030	RU	WNIALMI	Recipient	Bilateral	Susceptibility of quercus robur against damage by biotic and abiotic factors	Completed	1994	1995	Scientific/research		
DE031	RU	WNIALMI	Recipient	Bilateral	Pine breeding - improving the tolerance against dryness	Completed	1994	1995	Scientific/research		
DE037	RU	Moskow State University, Inst. of Forest Soil Science	Recipient	Bilateral	Monitoring of water and element cycling and climatologic conditions of forest ecosystem at CFBR, Russia	Completed	1991	0	Seminar/workshop	Scientific/research	Know-how transfer
DE037	RU	Russian Academy of Science, Inst. of Evolutionary Ecology	Recipient								
DE037	RU	Central Forest Biospere Reservation	Recipient								
DE043	RU	Forest Institute of the Russian Academy of Science	Recipient	Bilateral	Growth and structure of selected coniferous species in parts of Russia and easten Germany *	In planning	1996	1999	Scientific/research		
DE045	RU	Institute for Paper and Pulp	Recipient	Bilateral	Analysis on the paper and pulp markets	In planning	0	0	Scientific/research		
DE056	RU	All Russian Res. and Information Centre for Forest Res. of the Russ. Fed.	Recipient	Bilateral	German-Russian cooperation in agricultural research, THEMA 8	Completed	1989	0	Scientific/research	Know-how transfer	Other
DE057	RU	Institute of Forest SB RAS	Recipient	Bilateral	Growth and tree-ring-structure of coniferous species		0	0	Scientific/research	Know-how transfer	
DE065	RU	Moskauer Staatsuniversität des Waldes	Recipient	Bilateral	Long time development in requirements on power saws in the Moscow Region	Completed	1996	0	Scientific/research	Know-how transfer	
DE066	RU	Technological Institute	Recipient	Bilateral	Wood harvesting and timber industry in East Sibiria/Russia	Completed	1996	1997	Scientific/research		
DE067	RU	Kaunas - Akademija, LZUA, Litauen	Recipient	Bilateral	Analyzing of the framework and recommendations for founding of a Joint venture	Completed	1994	1995	Scientific/research		
DE075	RU	Technical Academy of Forestry	Recipient	Bilateral	Studies of change in forestry of the eastern part of Germany	In planning	1995	1996	Study tour		

H3 Projects, Recipient Country: *Russia (continued)*

Project ID		Organization	Position	Cooperation	Title	Status	From/in	To	Type 1	Type 2	Type 3
DE078	RU	All Russian Institute of Education in Forestry	Recipient	Bilateral	Advisory Seminar for Russian forest experts	Completed	1996	0	Seminar/workshop	Know-how transfer	
DE083	RU	All-Russian Institute of Education in Forestry	Recipient	Bilateral	Measures in forest policy in the frame of general economic developments	Completed	1996	1997	Scientific/research		
DE087	RU	Forest Administration Region of Perm	Recipient	Bilateral	Training in forest and timber management	Completed	1996	0	Education/training		
DE142	RU	All-Russia Institute of Continuous Education (VIPKLKH)	Recipient	Bilateral	Forest Economics	Completed	1996	0	Seminar/workshop		
DE143	RU	All-Russia Institute of Continuous Education (VIPKLKH)	Recipient	Bilateral	Forest Economics	Completed	1997	0	Study tour	Know-how transfer	
DE144	RU	All-Russia Institute of Continuous Education (VIPKLKH)	Recipient	Bilateral	Forest Economics	Completed	1998	0	Seminar/workshop	Know-how transfer	
DE145	RU	All-Russia Institute of Continuous Education (VIPKLKH)	Recipient	Bilateral	Forest Economics	Completed	1999	0	Seminar/workshop	Know-how transfer	
DE146	RU	All-Russia Institute of Continuous Education (VIPKLKH)	Recipient	Bilateral	Forest Economics	Completed	2000	0	Seminar/workshop	Study tour	
DK029	RU		Recipient	Bilateral	Development of Ecotourism and Nature Protection in the Kaliningrad Region, Russia	Completed	1997	0	Know-how transfer	Education/training	
DK030	RU	Kaliningrad Regional Center for Environmental and Biological Education (CEBE)	Recipient	Bilateral	Modernization and Elaboretion of the Understanding of Environment and of Nature on Kaliningrad, Russia		1997	0	Education/training	Know-how transfer	
DK035	RU		Recipient	Bilateral	Contribution towards a more sustainable Russia - integrating protected areas in a regional context	Ongoing	0	0	Capacity building	Know-how transfer	
DK040	RU		Recipient		Valdai National Park: capacity building, sustainable tourism, nature-friendly forestry and local involvement	Ongoing	0	0	Capacity building		
DK041	RU		Recipient	Bilateral	Centre for Nature and Environment, St. Petersburg (Pushkin), Russian Federation	Ongoing	0	0	Education/training	Institutional development	
DK042	RU		Recipient	Bilateral	Development and strengthening of the Kaliningrao Eco-Centre, Russian Federation	Ongoing	0	0	Institutional development	Know-how transfer	
DK048	RU		Recipient	Bilateral	Towards sustainable management of Sebezsky National Park in Russian Federation	Ongoing	0	0	Study tour	Seminar/workshop	Capacity building
EF001	RU		Recipient	Multilateral	Growth Trend of European Forests	Completed	1996	0	Scientific/research		
EU002	RU	State Ecology Committee of the Republic of Buryatia	Recipient	Multilateral	Natural resources management in the Baikal water basin.	In planning	1996	1999	Capacity building	Policy/strategy	Know-how transfer
EU002	RU	Many institutions and industries in Baikal region	Recipient								
EU002	RU	Irkutsk Oblast Committee for Environment and Natural Resources	Recipient								

H3 Projects, Recipient Country: *Russia (continued)*

Project ID		Organization	Position	Cooperation	Title	Status	From/in	To	Type 1	Type 2	Type 3
EU003	RU	State Karelian Research Institute of Forest Industry	Recipient	Multilateral	Forest management in north-west Russia	In planning	1996	1997	Capacity building	Policy/strategy	
EU003	RU	Scientific Research and Information Centre for Forest Resources	Recipient								
EU003	RU	Karelian Ministry of Industry, Transport and Communication	Recipient								
EU003	RU	Federal Forest Service of Russia	Recipient								
EU003	RU	Karellesprom	Recipient								
EU003	RU	State Forestry Committee of the Republic of Karelia	Recipient								
FI027	RU	State Forestry Committee	Recipient	Bilateral	Preparation of the Implementation Phase of the Forestry Development Programme in the Republic of Karelia in Rus.Fed	Completed	1995	1996	Capacity building		
FI028	RU	State Forestry Committee	Recipient	Bilateral	Karelian Forest Map Information System	Completed	1993	1996	Education/training	Technical development	Know-how transfer
FI029	RU	State Forestry Committee, Petrozavodsk Forest District	Recipient	Bilateral	Modernisation of Vilga Nursery in the Republic of Karelia in Russian Federation	Completed	1995	1996	Education/training	Technical development	Know-how transfer
FI030	RU	State Forestry Committee, Lahdenpohja Forest District	Recipient	Bilateral	Modernisation of Lahdenpohja Nursery in the Republic of Karelia in Russian Federation	Completed	1995	1997	Education/training	Technical development	Know-how transfer
FI031	RU	State Forestry Committee	Recipient	Bilateral	Vocational guidance in the field of forestry in Segezha in the Republic of Karelia	Completed	1992	1996	Education/training	Know-how transfer	
FI031	RU	Segezha Forestry District	Recipient								
FI032	RU	State Forestry Committee	Recipient	Bilateral	Circular sawing courses in the Republic of Karelia	Completed	1993	1995	Education/training	Know-how transfer	
FI033	RU	Ministry of Agriculture	Recipient	Bilateral	Consultation of the private forestry management in the Republic of Karelia	Completed	1993	1998	Education/training	Capacity building	Know-how transfer
FI034	RU	State Forestry Committee	Recipient	Bilateral	Cooperation between Kuusamo and Paanajärvi National Park in the Republic of Karelia	Completed	1994	1995	Capacity building	Know-how transfer	
FI034	RU	Paanajärvi National Park	Recipient								
FI035	RU	St. Petersburg Forest Technical Academy	Recipient	Bilateral	Effects of forestry in the Karelian Isthmus in Russian Federation	Completed	1995	0	Scientific/research	Know-how transfer	
FI036	RU	State Forestry Committee	Recipient	Bilateral	Forest harvesting and round wood export in North-west Russia	Completed	1995	1996	Other- Study (Assessment)		
FI037	RU	City of Kovdor	Recipient	Bilateral	Development of training in forestry and forestry-based economy in Kovdor in the Murmansk Region	Completed	1994	1995	Education/training	Capacity building	Know-how transfer
FI038	RU	Arctic Drev, Zelenoborsky Saw Mill	Recipient	Bilateral	Planning and execution of the acquisition of timber to the Zelenoborsk Saw Mill.	Completed	1995	1996	Capacity building	Know-how transfer	
FI039	RU	St. Petersburg Academy of Forestry	Recipient	Multilateral	Planning of the Lisino International Forestry Training Center in St. Petersburg	Completed	1994	1996	Education/training	Scientific/research	Capacity building

H3 Projects, Recipient Country: *Russia (continued)*

Project ID		Organization	Position	Cooperation	Title	Status	From/in	To	Type 1	Type 2	Type 3
FI040	RU	Karelian Forest Research Institute	Recipient	Bilateral	Thinning research in Russian Karelia	Ongoing	1991	2005	Scientific/research		
FI041	RU	Segezha Forestry District	Recipient	Bilateral	Development of silvicultural and timber harvesting training in the Republic of Karelia	Completed	1994	1996	Education/training	Technical development	Know-how transfer
FI041	RU	State Forestry Committee	Recipient								
FI042	RU	Petrozavodsk Pedagogic Institute	Recipient	Bilateral	Training cooperation in natural sciences in the Republic of Karelia	Completed	1994	1996	Education/training	Capacity building	
FI043	RU	Russian 4 H-Association	Recipient	Trilateral	Extending 4 H Ativities in the Republic of Karelia and the Murmansk region	Completed	1994	2000	Education/training		
FI043	RU	FSSCY Murmansk	Donor								
FI044	RU	Lenpromles Holding Company	Recipient	Bilateral	Land use and forestry planning project of the AOOT Kirovsk Lespromhos in Leningrad region.	Completed	1995	1996	Capacity building	Know-how transfer	
FI045	RU	Petrozavodsk Forestry Institute	Recipient	Bilateral	Effects of land use history on biodiversity in Russian Northern Boreal Forests	Completed	1993	1995	Scientific/research		
FI046	RU	Ministry of Ecology and Nature Resources	Recipient	Bilateral	Environmental Data System in the neighbouring areas, in Estonia and Russia	Completed	1994	1995	Technical development	Know-how transfer	
FI047	RU		Recipient	Multilateral	Conference on climate change, biodiversity and boreal forest ecosystems	Completed	1995	0	Seminar/workshop	Scientific/research	
FI047	RU		Recipient								
FI047	RU		Recipient								
FI048	RU	North-west Management Enterprise, Lesproject	Recipient	Bilateral	Ecological monitoring of forests in south-eastern Finland and in the Leningrad region	Completed	1991	1996	Scientific/research		
FI048	RU	Russian Academy of Science, Komarov Botanical Institute	Recipient								
FI049	RU	Russian Academy of Science, Karelian Research Centre	Recipient	Bilateral	Ecological monitoring of forest in south-eastern Finland and Kainuu region and in Karelia, Russian Federation	Completed	1991	1996	Scientific/research	Scientific/research	
FI050	RU	Institute of Limnology, Academy of Sciences	Recipient	Multilateral	Lake Ladoga Symposium (2nd international symposium)	In planning	1996	0	Seminar/workshop		
FI050	RU		Recipient								
FI050	RU	Karelian Research Centre	Recipient								
FO010	RU	Russian Inst. of Forest Specialists Education and Training	Recipient	Multilateral	IUFRO/SPDC travel grants	Completed	1995	0	Other (travel grant)		
FO010	RU	Komarov Botanical Institute	Recipient	Multilateral	IUFRO/SPDC travel grants	Completed	1995	0	Other (travel grant)		
FO010	RU	Federal Forest Service	Recipient								
FO010	RU	All Russian Inst. of Silviculture and Mechanization of Forestry	Recipient								
FR011	RU	International Forest Institute	Recipient	Bilateral	Use of remote sensing data and geographical information system for inventory and follow-up of Russian forests	Completed	1994	0	Technical development		

H3 Projects, Recipient Country: *Russia (continued)*

Project ID		Organization	Position	Cooperation	Title	Status	From/in	To	Type 1	Type 2	Type 3
GB004	RU		Recipient	Bilateral	European Community's Mission to the Russian Federation	Completed	1991	0	Study tour		
GB007	RU	Russian Federal Forestry Service	Recipient	Bilateral	Meschera National Park/North Scotland Exchange	Completed	1994	1995	Study tour		
GB015	RU	Federal Forest Service	Recipient		Sustainable Forestry Pilot Programme	Completed	1997	0	Technical development		Capacity building
GB017	RU	Federal Forestry Service	Recipient	Bilateral	FC/FFS Collaborative Project	Completed	1994	1997	Study tour	Seminar/workshop	
GB019	RU		Recipient	Bilateral	Creating a policy framework for National Parks	Ongoing	1999	2001	Policy/strategy		
GB021	RU	Federal Forest Service	Recipient	Bilateral	Russian British Sustainable Forest Management Planning Exercise	Postponed	2001	2001	Seminar/workshop	Technical development	
GB032	RU	Siberian Ecologica Fund	Recipient	Bilateral	Funding for 2 Siberians to participate in the UN Climate Change Convention in Kyoto	Completed	1998	1999	Seminar/workshop		
GB032	RU	Scientists for Global Responsibility	Recipient	Bilateral	Funding for 2 Siberians to participate in the UN Climate Change Convention in Kyoto	Completed	1998	1999	Seminar/workshop		
LI003	RU	Uralian Academy of Forestry	Recipient	Bilateral	Processes and techniques in multi-functional alpine forests	Completed	2000	2000	Scientific/research		
LT036	RU		Donor	Multilateral	International meeting of specialists on forest inventory and management		1997	0	Education/training		
NO001	RU		Recipient	Bilateral	Forest/Sawmilling Industry in the Archangel region	Completed	1995	0	Technical development		
NO002	RU		Recipient	Bilateral	Forestry-vacational training and trade of sawnwood in Vologda, Russian Fed.	Completed	1995	0	Education/training		
NO003	RU		Recipient	Bilateral	Logging operation in Pertominsk, Russian Fed.	Completed	1995	0	Technical development		
NO007	RU	Petrohouse A7S.	Recipient	Bilateral	Joint venture, establishing sawmill for export	Completed	1996	0			
NO008	RU	XL KEM, Proletarskii Prospect 21, Karelen.	Recipient	Multilateral	Beloporotsk - Kem River; Joint Norwegian, Finnish and Russian venture, Forest operation	Completed	1996	0			
NO009	RU	Rassvet	Recipient	Bilateral	Joint venture, establishment of a furniture factory, training project	Completed	1996	0	Education/training		
NO010	RU	Nizhny Novgorod	Recipient	Bilateral	Nizhny Novgorod; Joint venture, house production - training	Completed	1996	0	Education/training		
NO011	RU	Beverly Polska, cesary Kaczmarek	Recipient	Bilateral	Koscierzyna; Community production of house construction elements - windows.	Completed	1996	0			
NO012	RU	Pandestor AS	Recipient	Bilateral	Archangel; Joint venture forestry project. Investments and training project	Completed	1997	0	Education/training		
NO013	RU		Recipient	Bilateral	North-West region; Porject on establishing a housing element factory	Completed	1997	0	Technical assistance		
NO014	RU		Recipient	Bilateral	Verkhnetulomskij - Murmansk; Sawmill establishment project	Completed	1997	0	Education/training		
NO015	RU		Recipient	Bilateral	Kaliningrad; Quality insurance on planned bio-pellet production	Completed	1997	0	Education/training	Capacity building	
NO018	RU		Recipient	Bilateral	"Guidelines for environmentally sound forestry in the boreal forests of north-western Russia".	Completed	1996	1998	Policy/strategy		
NO019	RU		Donor	Bilateral	Bilateral environment protection cooperation between Norway and Russia--on the pollution effect on terrestrial ecosystems		0	0	Scientific/research	Other: cooperation	
NO020	RU	Krasnoyarsk Kray, Khabarovsk Kray, and Vologda region	Recipient	Trilateral	"Preparatory activities for the sustainable forestry pilot project"		1997	0	Policy/strategy		

H3 Projects, Recipient Country: *Russia (continued)*

Project ID		Organization	Position	Cooperation	Title	Status	From/in	To	Type 1	Type 2	Type 3
NO021	RU	Vologda, north-west Russia	Recipient	Bilateral	Joint venture on forest ownership and forest operation--Vologda, north-west Russia	Ongoing	0	0			
NO022	RU	Chereprovetz Les	Recipient	Bilateral	Joint venture with Chereprovetz Les on log trading	Ongoing	0	0			
RU001	RU	NIPIEIlesprom	Donor	Bilateral	Programme of restructuring the forest and forest products sector of the Republic of Komi, 1997.	Completed	1997	1997	Policy/strategy	Other	
RU001	RU	Republic of Komi	Recipient	Bilateral	Programme of restructuring the forest and forest products sector of the Republic of Komi, 1997.	Completed	1997	1997	Policy/strategy	Other	
RU002	RU	NIPIEIlesprom	Donor	Bilateral	Programme of restucturing the forest and forest products sector if Korov region	Completed	1997	1997	Policy/strategy	Other	
RU002	RU	Korov Region	Recipient	Bilateral	Programme of restucturing the forest and forest products sector if Korov region	Completed	1997	1997	Policy/strategy	Other	
RU003	RU	Republic of Bashkortostan	Recipient	Bilateral	Programme of restructuring the forest and forest products sector of the Republic of Bashkortostan	Completed	1997	1997	Policy/strategy	Other	
RU003	RU	NIPIEIlesprom	Donor	Bilateral	Programme of restructuring the forest and forest products sector of the Republic of Bashkortostan	Completed	1997	1997	Policy/strategy	Other	
RU004	RU	NIPIEIlesprom	Donor	Bilateral	Programme of restructuring the forest and forest products sector of the Russian Federation		1999	1999	Policy/strategy	Other	
RU004	RU		Recipient	Bilateral	Programme of restructuring the forest and forest products sector of the Russian Federation		1999	1999	Policy/strategy	Other	
RU005	RU	NIPIEIlesprom	Donor	Bilateral	Programme of restructuring the forest and forest products sector of Vologda region	Completed	1999	1999			
RU005	RU	Vologda region	Recipient	Bilateral	Programme of restructuring the forest and forest products sector of Vologda region	Completed	1999	1999			
RU006	RU	NIPIEIlesprom	Donor	Bilateral	Sectoral purpose-oriented programme of furthering employment of population in the forest and forest products sector	Completed	1997	2000	Policy/strategy		
RU006	RU		Recipient								
RU007	RU	NIPIEIlesprom	Donor	Bilateral	Programme of restructuring the forest and forest products sector of the Udmurt Republic	Completed	1998	1998	Policy/strategy	Other	
RU007	RU	Udmurt Republic	Recipient								
RU008	RU	NIPIEIlesprom	Donor		Study of forest cargos transportation flows and elaboration of measures, aimed at reducing transportation costs	Completed	1999	1999	Technical development	Policy/strategy	
RU008	RU		Recipient								
RU009	RU	NIPIEIlesprom	Donor	Bilateral	Analysis of state of integration processes in the forest and forest products sector of Russia	Completed	1999	1999	Technical development	Policy/strategy	
RU009	RU		Recipient								
RU010	RU		Recipient	Bilateral	System of management of production costs at enterprises of the forest and forest products sector, aimed at their minimization	Completed	1999	1999	Policy/strategy	Technical development	

H3 Projects, Recipient Country: *Russia (continued)*

Project ID		Organization	Position	Cooperation	Title	Status	From/in	To	Type 1	Type 2	Type 3
RU010	RU	NIPIEllesprom	Donor								
RU011	RU	NIPIEllesprom	Recipient	Bilateral	International Conference "Strategy for developing the forest and forest products sector of the Russian Federation in XXI century"		2000	2000	Conference		
RU011	RU	NIPIEllesprom	Donor								
RU012	EB	EBRB	Donor		Pilot Project on Sustainable Forestry -- assistance from EBRD	Ongoing	2001	0	Institutional development		
RU012	RU		Recipient								
SE004	RU	Federal Forest Service of Russia	Recipient	Bilateral	Two-week study tour	Completed	1995	0	Study tour		
SE012	RU		Recipient	Bilateral	Study tour on "General forestry conditions in Sweden"	Completed	1993	0	Study tour		
SE019	RU	Novgorod Region	Recipient	Bilateral	Forest cadastre	Completed	1994	0	Capacity building		
SE030	RU		Recipient	Bilateral	Wood field development -- a project in Lithuania, Russian Federation	Ongoing	2000	2004			
SE032	RU		Recipient	Bilateral	Training of Russian Chief Foresters	Ongoing	2000	2002	Education/training		
SE033	RU		Recipient	Bilateral	Pskov Model Forest -- a project in Russian Federation	Ongoing	2001	2003			
UA004	RU		Donor	Multilateral	Legal, administrative and policy strategies for securing sustainable development of the forest sector in Russia, Belarus and Ukrain (INTAS programme)	Completed	1996	1998	Policy/strategy	Institutional development	

H3 Projects, Recipient Country: *Slovakia*

Project ID		Organization	Position	Cooperation	Title	Status	From/in	To	Type 1	Type 2	Type 3
AT003	SK	Ministerstvo Podohospodarstva	Recipient	Bilateral	Study Tour--Forest policy in Austria	Completed	1993	0	Study tour		
CZ025	SK	Slovak Academy of Sciences, Institute of Landscape Ecology	Recipient	Multilateral	Evaluation of ozone air pollution and its phytotoxic potential in the Carpathian forests	Completed	1997	0	Scientific/research		
DE001	SK	Institute of Plant Genetics	Recipient	Bilateral	Scientific and technical cooperation between Saxonian and Slovakian Forestry Research Institutions	Completed	1995	0	Scientific/research		
DE001	SK	Forestry Faculty	Recipient								
DE001	SK	Forestry Research Institute	Recipient								
DE004	SK	Slowakian Association of Private Forest Owners	Recipient	Bilateral	Privatization of forest land	Completed	1993	0	Know-how transfer		
DE011	SK	University	Recipient	Bilateral	Modelling of Mortality Process in Forest Stands	Completed	1995	1996	Scientific/research		
DE017	SK	University Zvolen	Recipient	Bilateral	3rd Colloquium acustics 1996	In planning	1996	0	Seminar/workshop		
DE027	SK	Ustav pre Vychovu a Vzdelavanie	Recipient	Bilateral	Study tour on German forestry education system	Completed	1995	0	Study tour		
DE028	SK	Slovakian Ministry of Agriculture	Recipient	Bilateral	Round trip -- foresters in Bavaria	Completed	1995	0	Study tour		
DE036	SK	Slovakian Forest Research Institute, Zvolen, Slovakia	Recipient	Bilateral	Pests on oak and their enemies in the Western Carpathian mountains	Completed	1992	1995	Scientific/research		

H3 Projects, Recipient Country: *Slovakia (continued)*

Project ID		Organization	Position	Cooperation	Title	Status	From/in	To	Type 1	Type 2	Type 3
DE041	SK	Lehrstuhl für Forsteinrichtung und Geodasie	Donor	Bilateral	Identification of forest damages and qualification of their effects on the growth of forests	Completed	1992	1998	Scientific/research		
DE046	SK	Landwirtschaft ministerium	Donor	Bilateral	Quantification of forest damages' effects on growth and production with the help of GIS and biometrical models.	Completed	1992	0	Scientific/research		
DE046	SK	TU Zvolen	Recipient								
DE047	SK	TU Zvolen, University of Zvolen	Recipient	Multilateral	TEMPUS-Mobility-Project *	Completed	1994	1996	Education/training		
DE052	SK	University	Recipient	Multilateral	Technology for products from black locust (Robinia pseudoacacia)	Completed	1996	0	Scientific/research	Technical development	
DE054	SK	Chair of Forest Inventory and Geodesy	Recipient	Bilateral	Modelling mortality in single tree growth models	Completed	1995	1996	Scientific/research		
DE059	SK	Research institute for Forestry	Recipient	Multilateral	Differential diagnosing of oak damage in the Danub region	Completed	1992	1994	Scientific/research		
DE061	SK	Institute of Forest Ecology	Recipient	Bilateral	The role of forest reserves in conserving saproxylic invertebrates in oak and beech forest of central Slovakia.	Completed	1996	0	Scientific/research		
DE063	SK	TU Zvolen, Department of Silviculture	Recipient	Multilateral	Joint workshops BRNO-THARANDT	Ongoing	0	0	Seminar/workshop	Seminar/workshop	
DE064	SK	State Forest Products Research Institute	Recipient	Multilateral	Cost action E2 wood durability	Completed	1994	1998	Scientific/research		
DE073	SK	Forest Research Institute	Recipient	Multilateral	EUROPGEN IPGRI Meeting on Hardwoods	Completed	1996	0	Seminar/workshop	Scientific/research	Know-how transfer
DE080	SK	State Forest Administration	Recipient	Bilateral	Improvement of forest management	In planning	1996	0	Seminar/workshop		
DE088	SK	Akademie der Wissenschaften	Recipient	Multilateral	Conservation of genetic resources in forest ecosystems	In planning	1996	0	Scientific/research	Technical development	Know-how transfer
DE088	SK	Forstl. Forschungsanst. Zvolen	Recipient								
DE088	SK	Universität Zvolen	Recipient								
EU001	SK	Min. of the Environment - Nature & Landscape Protection Dev. Dept.	Recipient	Multilateral	Sustainable forestry and forest biodiversity conservation in central-eastem Europe	Completed	1998	2001	Scientific/research	Capacity building	Policy/strategy
FO005	SK	Forest Research Institute	Recipient	Multilateral	IUFRO/SPDC travel grants	Completed	1994	0	Other (travel grant)		
GB005	SK	P.J. Safárik University	Recipient	Multilateral	Control and East Slovak Mobility Project CESMOP / Training of Slovak students (TEMPUS Programme)	Completed	1994	1997	Education/training		
GB005	SK	University of Zvolen	Recipient								
GB026	SK	WWF (funded by World Bank)	Recipient	Bilateral	Various consultancy projects in Romania, Slovakia and Latvia on certification of forests.	Completed	2000	0	Seminar/workshop	Technical development	Know-how transfer
GB038	SK	Low Tatras National Park	Recipient	Bilateral	Support for National Parks	Suggested	1997	0	Technical development		
GR001	SK	Forest Research Institute	Recipient	Bilateral	Scientific and Technical Cooperation	In planning	1995	1996	Scientific/research		
IE005	SK	Softip Zarnovica S.R.O.	Recipient	Bilateral	Eurochambres - Industrial Training Attrachments 1995	Completed	1995	0	Education/training		
SE002	SK		Recipient	Trilateral	Study tour on "Evaluation of forest"	Completed	1995	0	Study tour		

H3 Projects, Recipient Country: *Slovakia (continued)*

Project ID		Organization	Position	Cooperation	Title	Status	From/in	To	Type 1	Type 2	Type 3
SE003	SK		Recipient	Bilateral	Forest policy, legislation and extension	Completed	1995	0	Know-how transfer		
SE018	SK		Recipient	Multilateral	Study tour on "Forestry"	Completed	1994	1994	Study tour		
SE027	SK	Ministry of Agriculture	Recipient	Bilateral	Study tour to follow-up of the two courses on "Training, Information in Estonia" and "Forest Mensuration and Evaluation" carried out in 1995.	Completed	1997	1997	Study tour	Education/training	
SK001	FA	Food and Agriculture Organization of the United Nations	Donor	Multilateral	Institution-building, framework conditions and policy infrastructure for sustainable development of forestry	In planning	1996	0	Seminar/workshop		
SK001	SK	Forest Research Institute	Donor								
UA005	SK		Donor	Multilateral	Effects of Air Pollution on Forests Health and Biodiversity in forests of the Carpathian Mountains (Programme of IUFRO-SPDC)	Completed	1997	2001	Scientific/research		
UA011	SK		Donor	Multilateral	Scientific background of reforestation and afforestation improvement activities in Carpathian mountains	Ongoing	2000	0	Scientific/research		

H3 Projects, Recipient Country: *Slovenia*

Project ID		Organization	Position	Cooperation	Title	Status	From/in	To	Type 1	Type 2	Type 3
AT016	SI	Biotechnical Faculty, University of Ljubljana	Recipient	Multilateral	Brown bears in Slovenia -- Potential and limitations in a cultivated landscape	Completed	1997	1999	Scientific/research	Education/training	Policy/strategy
AT017	SI	Gozdarski Institute Slovenije	Recipient	Trilateral	Population ecology of lynx and bear in Slovenia/Carynthia	Completed	1993	1997	Scientific/research	Know-how transfer	Education/training
AT018	SI	Slovenian Foresters Association	Recipient	Bilateral	Association of Private forest Landowners	Completed	1997	0	Know-how transfer		
AT028	SI		Recipient	Trilateral	Study Tour--Pannonia Meeting 1996	Completed	1996	0	Study tour		
DE042	SI	University Ljubljana	Recipient	Bilateral	Sustainable development of the Slovenian forestry sector	In planning	1996	1998	Scientific/research		
DE064	SI	Biotechn. Faculty	Recipient	Multilateral	Cost action E2 wood durability	Completed	1994	1998	Scientific/research		
EF001	SI		Recipient	Multilateral	Growth Trend of European Forests	Completed	1996	0	Scientific/research		
EU001	SI	Forestry Institute of Slovenia	Recipient	Multilateral	Sustainable forestry and forest biodiversity conservation in central-eastern Europe	Completed	1998	2001	Scientific/research	Capacity building	Policy/strategy
HR003	SI		Donor	Bilateral	Eco-system management in wood processing	In planning	1999	2002	Scientific/research		
HR003	SI		Recipient	Bilateral	Eco-system management in wood processing	In planning	1999	2002	Scientific/research		
HU004	SI	Slovenian Forestry Association	Donor	Bilateral	Study tou in Slovenia	Completed	1995	0	Study tour		
IE004	SI	Ministry of Environment and Physical Planning	Recipient	Trilateral	Technical Assistance to the Slovenian Ministry of Environment and Physical Planning	Ongoing	0	0	Policy/strategy		
SI001	SI	Gozdarski Institut Slovenije	Recipient	Multilateral	TEMPUS - Bioindication of forest site pollution	Completed	0	0	Seminar/workshop	Education/training	
SI001	DE	Institute for Systematic Botany	Donor								
SI001	GB	Department of Plant Sciences, University of Cambridge	Donor								

H3 Projects, Recipient Country: *Slovenia (continued)*

Project ID		Organization	Position	Cooperation	Title	Status	From/in	To	Type 1	Type 2	Type 3
SI001	AT	Institute of Plant Physiology, Karl-Franzens University	Donor								
SI001	SI	Agronomy Department, Biotechnical Faculty, University of Ljubljana	Recipient								
SI002	AT	Institute of Forest Ecology, UNI BOKU, Vienna	Donor	Bilateral	Oak decline in Slovenia	Completed	1993	1994	Scientific/research		
SI002	SI	Gozdarski Institut Slovenije	Donor								
SI002	SI	Ministry of Agriculture, Forestry and Food	Donor								
SI003	EU	European Commission -- Phare	Donor	Multilateral	Energy Conservation Strategy in Slovenia	Completed	1994	1995	Scientific/research		
SI003	SI	Institut Josef Stefan	Recipient								
SI003	SI	Gozdarski Institut Slovenije	Recipient								
SI004	SI	Gozdarski Institut Slovenije	Recipient	Bilateral	Study of endophytic fungal populations in the needles of Norway spruce (Picea abies)	In planning	3	0	Scientific/research		
SI004	GB	Biotechnical Centre, Cranfield University	Recipient	Bilateral							
SI004	GB	The British Counsil Slovenia	Donor	Bilateral							

H3 Projects, Recipient Country: *Ukraine*

Project ID		Organization	Position	Cooperation	Title	Status	From/in	To	Type 1	Type 2	Type 3
CZ026	UA	Ukrainian Research Inst. of Forestry	Recipient	Multilateral	Scenario analysis of sustainable wood production under different forest management regimes (SCEFORMA)	Ongoing	1998	2001	Scientific/research		
CZ027	UA		Recipient	Multilateral	GEF I - Restoration of Forest Ecosystems-- Global Environment Facility/Biodiversity Protection Project	Completed	1993	1997	Education/training	Financial assistance	Capacity building
DE014	UA	Lvov Institute of Forestry and Wood Technology	Recipient	Bilateral	Evaluation of genetic resources of beech for sustainable forest management	Completed	1995	0	Scientific/research		
DE029	UA	Ukrainian State Univ. of Forestry and Wood Technology	Recipient	Multilateral	Natural Resource Economies (NARECO), Tempus–Tacis Pre-Joint	Completed	1995	1996	Education/training	Technical development	Know-how transfer
DE089	UA	Ukrainian State University of Forestry and Wood Technology	Recipient	Multilateral	Natural Resource Economics (Tempus–Tacis pre-project)	Ongoing	0	0	Education/training	Know-how transfer	
DE090	UA	Ukrainian State University of Forestry and Wood Technology	Recipient	Multilateral	Environment and Natural Resource Economics (tempus-Tacis JEP)	Suggested	0	0	Education/training	Technical development	Know-how transfer
GB010	UA	Forest Ministry Enterprise "Zhitomirles"	Recipient	Bilateral	Ukrainian Inward Mission	Completed	1995	0	Study tour		
GB013	UA	Kiev city State Administration	Recipient	Bilateral	Establishment of cost-effective and efficient management of the city of Kiev's natural environment.	Completed	1995	1997	Know-how transfer	Technical development	

H3 Projects, Recipient Country: *Ukraine (continued)*

Project ID		Organization	Position	Cooperation	Title	Status	From/in	To	Type 1	Type 2	Type 3
GB028	UA	Ministry for Environment Protection	Recipient	Multilateral	Sustainable Tourism Development in Protected Areas	Completed	1997	1999	Capacity building		
GB034	UA		Recipient	Bilateral	Workshop on how NGOs can effectively use the UN system to promote environmental activities, with a special emphasis on freshwater issues	Completed	1998	1999	Seminar/workshop		
LI001	UA	State Committee of Forestry	Recipient	Bilateral	Practical training in sustainable use of alpine forests	Completed	2000	2000	Education/training	Technical development	Know-how transfer
LI002	UA	Biosphere Reserve	Recipient	Bilateral	Private forestry/agroforestry development	Completed	1998	1998	Study tour		
SE007	UA	Ministry of Forestry	Recipient	Bilateral	Two-weeks mission to Ukraine	Completed	1995	0	Seminar/workshop		
SE026	UA	Ministry of Forestry	Recipient	Bilateral	Study tour on "Introduction to Swedish forestry"	Completed	1996	1996	Study tour	Education/training	
SE034	UA		Recipient	Bilateral	Forest Sector Master Plan -- a project in Ukraine.	Ongoing	2001	2004			
TR004	UA		Recipient	Multilateral	Education/Training on erosion control, arid zone plantation and nursery techniques	Completed	2000	2000	Education/training		
UA001	US	International Centre of Ecological Programmes	Donor	Bilateral	Equipment supply for Ukrainian for Forest Health Monitoring Programme	Completed	1995	1996	Technical development		
UA001	UA	Institute of Forest Scientifica Research and Agroforestry Bonification	Recipient								
UA002	UA	Forest Ministry	Recipient	Bilateral	Study Tour to Sweden	Completed	1995	0	Study tour		
UA002	SE	National Forest Council	Donor								
UA002	SE	SIDA	Donor								
UA003	CA		Donor	Multilateral	International Cooperative Programme on the Assessment and Monitoring of Air Pollution Effects on Forests (ICP Forests), UN/ECE	Ongoing	1989	0	Scientific/research		
UA003	US		Donor								
UA003	UA		Recipient								
UA004	AT		Donor	Multilateral	Legal, administrative and policy strategies for securing sustainable development of the forest sector in Russia, Belarus and Ukrain (INTAS programme)	Completed	1996	1998	Policy/strategy	Institutional development	
UA004	DE		Donor								
UA004	RU		Donor								
UA004	EF		Donor								
UA004	UA		Recipient								
UA005	CZ		Donor	Multilateral	Effects of Air Pollution on Forests Health and Biodiversity in forests of the Carpathian Mountains (Programme of IUFRO-SPDC)	Completed	1997	2001	Scientific/research		
UA005	UA		Donor								
UA005	RO		Donor								
UA005	US		Donor								
UA005	SK		Donor								

H3 Projects, Recipient Country: *Ukraine (continued)*

Project ID		Organization	Position	Cooperation	Title	Status	From/in	To	Type 1	Type 2	Type 3
UA005	PL		Donor								
UA006	UA		Donor	Bilateral	Contribution to the Temperate and Boreal Forest Resources Assessment 2000 (TBFRA-2000) implemented by the Timber section of the UNECE		0	0		Other	
UA006	EC	Economic Commission for Europe	Recipient								
UA007	SE		Donor	Bilateral	Strategic plan of forest sector development in Ukraine	Completed	1998	2000	Technical development	Institutional development	
UA007	UA		Recipient								
UA008	CH		Donor	Bilateral	Forest certification of 4 forestry enterprises under FSC scheme	Completed	2000	2001	Institutional development		
UA008	UA		Recipient								
UA009	CZ		Donor	Multilateral	Scenario analysis of sustainable wood production under different forest management regimes (SCEFORMA) (INCO-Copernicus programme)	Ongoing	1998	2001	Education/training	Technical assistance	
UA009	UA		Recipient								
UA009	HU		Donor								
UA009	EF	European Forest Institute	Donor								
UA009	UA		Donor								
UA009	NL		Donor								
UA009	PL		Donor								
UA010	UA		Recipient	Bilateral	European forest genetic resources programme (EUFORGEN)	Completed	1998	0	Technical development	Scientific/research	
UA011	PL		Partner	Multilateral	Scientific background of reforestation and afforestation improvement activities in Carpathian mountains	Ongoing	2000	0	Scientific/research		
UA011	HU		Partner								
UA011	RO		Partner								
UA011	SK		Partner								
UA011	UA		Partner								
UA011	UA		Partner								
UA012	UA		Recipient	Bilateral	Nature values in the East and West: biodiversity - native forests - protection territories.	Ongoing	2000	0			
UA012	CH		Donor								
UA013	UA		Recipient	Multilateral	International conference "Challenges for Forestry in Central European Countires and Newly Independent States: breaking through in the EU".	In planning	0	0	Conference		
UA013	EF	European Forest Institute	Donor								
UA013	NL		Donor								
UA014	UA		Recipient	Bilateral	Ukrainian Forestry Web-page for Forest Information Services Network for Europe (FINE)	In planning	2001	2003	Education/training		

H3 Projects, Recipient Country: *Ukraine (continued)*

Project ID		Organization	Position	Cooperation	Title	Status	From/in	To	Type 1	Type 2	Type 3
UA014	EF	European Forest Institute	Donor	Bilateral	Ukrainian Forestry Web-page for Forest Information Services Network for Europe (FINE)	In planning	2001	2003	Education/training		
UA015	EC	UN-ECE	Recipient	Bilateral	Ukrainian studies of European forest sector outlook studies (EFSOS)	In planning	2001	2003 "			
UA015	UA		Donor	Bilateral	Ukrainian studies of European forest sector outlook studies (EFSOS)	In planning	2001	2003 "			

H3 Projects, Non-signatory Countries: *Armenia*

Project ID	Organization	Position	Cooperation	Title	Status	From/in	To	Type 1	Type 2	Type 3
AM001	FAO	Donor	Multilateral	Armenian forest sector development (FAO Technical Cooperation Programme ARM/4451/6612 (1994-1997) TCP)	Completed	1994	1997	Capacity building		
	ARMFOREST Association	Recipient				1994	1997	Capacity building		
AM002	World Bank	Donor	Multilateral	National Environmental Action Plan (NEAP) 1998-1999	Completed	1998	1999	Capacity building		
		Recipient			Completed	1998	1999	Capacity building		
AM003	SIDA	Donor	Bilateral	Forest Resources Assessment (SIDA) 1998-1999	Completed	1998	1999	Institutional development	Education/training	
		Recipient			Completed	1998	1999	Institutional development	Education/training	
AM004		Donor	Bilateral	Development of the Forest Certification Standard for Armenia (UK FCO) 2000.	Completed	2000	2000	Policy/strategy		
		Recipient			Completed	2000	2000	Policy/strategy		
AM005	World Bank (under TACIS project)	Donor	Multilateral	Joint Environmental Programme (JEP-06, TACIS)	Ongoing	0	0	Capacity building	Financial assistance	
		Recipient			Ongoing	0	0	Capacity building	Financial assistance	
GB025	Forest Research & Experimental	Recipient	Bilateral	Developments of a Forest Certification Standard for Armenia	Completed	2000	2000	Capacity building	Know-how transfer	

H3 Projects, Non-signatory Countries: *Azerbaijan*

Project ID	Organization	Position	Cooperation	Title	Status	From/in	To	Type 1	Type 2	Type 3
TR001		Recipient	Multilateral	Region cooperation meeting on forestry.	Completed	1997	0	Seminar/workshop		
TR002		Recipient	Multilateral	Recycling, energy and market interactions	Completed	1998	0	Seminar/workshop		
TR004		Recipient	Multilateral	Education/Training on erosion control, arid zone plantation and nursery techniques	Completed	2000	2000	Education/training		

H3 Projects, Non-signatory Countries: *Bosnia and Herzogovina*

Project ID	Organization	Position	Cooperation	Title	Status	From/in	To	Type 1	Type 2	Type 3
BA001	European Commission	Donor	Bilateral	Forestry Project in Bosnia and Herzegovina (Project of the World Bank)	Ongoing	0	2001	Institutional development	Capacity building	Financial assistance
BA001	Italy	Donor								
BA001	Norway	Donor								
BA001	World Bank	Donor								

H3 Projects, Non-signatory Countries: *Bosnia and Herzegovina (continued)*

Project ID	Organization	Position	Cooperation	Title	Status	From/in	To	Type 1	Type 2	Type 3
BA001	Bosnia and Herzegovina	Recipient								
BA002	NOVUA FRONTIERA, (an NGO)	Donor	Bilateral	Reforestation, training and education, as well as the means for seed production (Assistance from NOVUA, Italy)		0	0	Education/training	Technical development	Capacity building
BA002	Bosnia and Herzegovina	Recipient								
BA003		Donor		Reforestation projects (donation of "LORA", Italy)	Completed	0	0	Capacity building		
BA003	Bosnia and Herzegovina	Recipient								
BA004		Donor	Bilateral	Education of personnel for sustainable projects in forestry (aid of the Japanese government)	In planning	0	0	Education/training		
BA004	Bosnia and Herzegovina	Recipient	Bilateral	Education of personnel for sustainable projects in forestry (aid of the Japanese government)	In planning	0	0	Education/training		
EU001	Fed. Min. of Agriculture, Water management and Forestry	Recipient	Multilateral	Sustainable forestry and forest biodiversity conservation in central-eastern Europe	In planning	1997	1998	Scientific/research	Capacity building	Policy/strategy
IT002	Bosnia and Herzegovina	Recipient	Multilateral	Assistance to the Forestry Project of Bosnia and Herzegovina (BA-PE-45134)	Ongoing	1999	2001	Education/training	Scientific/research	Technical development

H3 Projects, Non-signatory Countries: *Georgia*

Project ID	Organization	Position	Cooperation	Title	Status	From/in	To	Type 1	Type 2	Type 3
AT011	State Department of Forest Management	Recipient	Multilateral	Study Tour--Forest policy in Austria	Completed	1997	0	Study tour		
GB023	Mtsketz Mtianeti Region	Recipient	Bilateral	Localized study to assess the potential of plant material grown for medical & herbal purposes and to recommend improvements to sheep farming industry	Completed	1999	2000	Technical development		
GE001	WB Inst.Dev.Fund	Donor	Multilateral	National Forestry Strategy	Completed	1997	0	Policy/strategy	Institutional development	
GE002	Government of Georgia	Recipient	Multilateral	Forest Develoment Programme for Georgia	In planning	0	0	Policy/strategy	Institutional development	Capacity building

H3 Projects, Non-signatory Countries: *Kyrgystan*

Project ID	Organization	Position	Cooperation	Title	Status	From/in	To	Type 1	Type 2	Type 3
CH004	Institute of Sylviculture	Recipient	Bilateral	Programme of development in the forest sector, Phase I -- Kyrgyzstan	Completed	1995	1997	Education/training	Policy/strategy	
DE039	Institute of Forestry, Bischkek	Recipient	Bilateral	Preservation and rejuvenating of walnut tree stands	In planning	0	0	Scientific/research		
TR001		Recipient	Multilateral	Region cooperation meeting on forestry.	Completed	1997	0	Seminar/workshop		
TR002		Recipient	Multilateral	Recycling, energy and market interactions	Completed	1998	0	Seminar/workshop		
TR004		Recipient	Multilateral	Education/Training on erosion control, arid zone plantation and nursery techniques	Completed	2000	2000	Education/training		

H3 Projects, Non-signatory Countries: *Kazakhstan*

Project ID	Organization	Position	Cooperation	Title	Status	From/in	To	Type 1	Type 2	Type 3
TR001		Recipient	Multilateral	Region cooperation meeting on forestry.	Completed	1997	0	Seminar/workshop		
TR004		Recipient	Multilateral	Education/Training on erosion control, arid zone plantation and nursery techniques	Completed	2000	2000	Education/training		

H3 Projects, Non-signatory Countries: *The FYR of Macedonia*

Project ID	Organization	Position	Cooperation	Title	Status	From/in	To	Type 1	Type 2	Type 3
EU001	Min. of Agriculture, Forestry & Water Management	Recipient	Multilateral	Sustainable forestry and forest biodiversity conservation in central-eastern Europe	Completed	1998	2001	Scientific/research	Capacity building	Policy/strategy
MK001	Instituto di Patologia Vegetale, Universita degli Studi di Milano	Donor	Trilateral	Vegetative compatibility types of Cryphonectria parasitica in the Republic of Macedonia	Suggested	1997	2001	Scientific/research	Seminar/workshop	
MK001	Swiss Federal Institute for Forest, Snow, and Landscape	Donor								
MK001	Faculty of Forestry, Skopje	Recipient								
MK002	Faculty of Forestry, Skopje	Recipient	Multilateral	Influence of airpollution and changes of some climatological elements on dieback process in oak and fir forests	In planning	1997	2000	Scientific/research	Education/training	Capacity building
MK002		Donor								
MK002		Donor								
MK002		Donor								
MK002		Donor								
MK002		Donor								
MK002		Donor								
MK003	Faculty of Forestry	Recipient	Trilateral	The thinning technique in forest cultures in Republic of Macedonia	In planning	1997	2002	Technical development	Capacity building	
MK003		Donor								
MK003		Donor								
MK004	British Council (International Associations of Botanic Gardens) (Spain)	Donor	Trilateral	First European Botanic Garden Conference	Suggested	1997	0	Education/training	Technical assistance	
MK004	Faculty of Forestry	Recipient								
MK004	British Council (Botanical Gardens Conservation International)	Donor								
MK005		Donor	Bilateral	Biological control of Thaumatopoea pityocampa Schiff	Completed	1997	2000	Scientific/research		
MK005	Forest Faculty	Recipient								
MK005		Donor								
MK006	(SAAB) Groupement suisse pour les regions des montagnes	Donor	Bilateral	Selection of the seed plantations of more important forest trees in Rep. of Macedonia	Suggested	1997	1998	Scientific/research		
MK006	Faculty of Forestry	Recipient								
MK007	Faculty of Forestry	Recipient	Multilateral	Productivity of pure even-aged beech stands in the Republic of Macedonia	In planning	1997	1997	Scientific/research		
MK008	Ministry of Forestry	Donor	Bilateral	Survey of macedonian dendroflora 2. The state of the forest genoond in Macedonia	Suggested	1997	0	Seminar/workshop		

H3 Projects, Non-signatory Countries: *Tajikistan*

Project ID		Organization	Position	Cooperation	Title	Status	From/in	To	Type 1	Type 2	Type 3
TR001			Recipient	Multilateral	Region cooperation meeting on forestry.	Completed	1997	0	Seminar/workshop		

H3 Projects, Non-signatory Countries: *Uzbekistan*

Project ID		Organization	Position	Cooperation	Title	Status	From/in	To	Type 1	Type 2	Type 3
TR001			Recipient	Multilateral	Region cooperation meeting on forestry.	Completed	1997	0	Seminar/workshop		
TR002			Recipient	Multilateral	Recycling, energy and market interactions	Completed	1998	0	Seminar/workshop		

H3 Projects, Non-signatory Countries: *Republic of Moldova (observer)*

Project ID		Organization	Position	Cooperation	Title	Status	From/in	To	Type 1	Type 2	Type 3
MD001		Finnish Forest and Park Service	Donor	Bilateral	Strategy for sustainable development of the forest sector in the Republic of Moldova	Completed	1998	1998	Policy/strategy		
MD001		State Forest Service	Recipient								
NO017			Recipient	Bilateral	"PRIRODA" Environmental technology programme	Ongoing	0	0	Technical assistance		

H3 Projects, International Organisations: *CEI Bois*

Project ID		Organization	Position	Cooperation	Title	Status	From/in	To	Type 1	Type 2	Type 3
FR001	CE	Confederation Européene des Industries du Bois	Donor	Multilateral	Cooperation in mechanical wood-processing sector	Completed	1995	0	Seminar/workshop		

H3 Projects, International Organisations: *UNDP*

Project ID		Organization	Position	Cooperation	Title	Status	From/in	To	Type 1	Type 2	Type 3
AL003	DP	United Nations Development Programme	Donor	Multilateral	Projects under planning in cooperation with ICP Forest, ECE, World Bank, FAO, UNDP, UNEP, GEF, IUFRO, EBRD on the areas mentioned under the "contents"	In planning	0	0			
BG006	DP	United Nations Development Programme	Donor	Multilateral	National Biodiversity Conservation Plan, Sofia 2000 (UNDP/GEF/MOEW)	Ongoing	1999	2003	Policy/strategy		

H3 Projects, International Organisations: *EBRD*

Project ID		Organization	Position	Cooperation	Title	Status	From/in	To	Type 1	Type 2	Type 3
RU012	EB	EBRB	Donor	Multilateral	Pilot Project on Sustainable Forestry -- assistance from EBRD	Ongoing	2001	0	Institutional development		

H3 Projects, International Organisations: *EU*

Project ID		Organization	Position	Cooperation	Title	Status	From/in	To	Type 1	Type 2	Type 3
BA001	EU	European Commission	Donor	Multilateral	Forestry Project in Bosnia and Herzegovina (Project of the World Bank)	Ongoing	0	2001	Institutional development	Capacity building	Financial assistance
CZ010	EU	EC -- Phare	Donor	Multilateral	Czech forestry sector study	Completed	1994	1995	Policy/strategy		
DE047	EU	EC -- TEMPUS Office	Donor	Multilateral	TEMPUS-Mobility-Project *	Completed	1994	1996	Education/training		
DE052	EU	European Community	Donor	Multilateral	Technology for products from black locust (Robinia pseudoacacia)	Completed	1996	0	Scientific/research	Technical development	
DE064	EU	EU - DG XII	Donor	Multilateral	Cost action E2 wood durability	Completed	1994	1998	Scientific/research		
DE089	EU	European Training Foundation	Donor	Multilateral	Natural Resource Economics (Tempus-Tacis pre-project)	Ongoing	0	0	Education/training	Know-how transfer	
DE090	EU	European Training Foundation	Donor	Multilateral	Environment and Natural Resource Economics (tempus-Tacis JEP)	Suggested	0	0	Education/training	Technical development	Know-how transfer
DE100	EU	EU - Tempus Phare	Donor	Multilateral	Development of forestry education as a profession for the protection of environment	Ongoing	0	0	Seminar/workshop	Education/training	Capacity building

H3 Projects, International Organisations: *EU (continued)*

Project ID		Organization	Position	Cooperation	Title	Status	From/in	To	Type 1	Type 2	Type 3
EE007	EU	EC Phar/Tacis CBC Project facility	Donor	Bilateral	Establishment of foundation Private Forest Centre	Completed	1998	2000	Seminar/workshop	Education/training	Policy/strategy
EU001	SI	Forestry Institute of Slovenia	Recipient	Multilateral	Sustainable forestry and forest biodiversity conservation in central-eastern Europe	Completed	1998	2001	Scientific/research	Capacity building	
EU001	BG	Min. of Environment and Waters (National Nature protection Service)mS. mIRA mILEVA	Recipient								
EU001	MK	Min. of Agriculture, Forestry & Water Management	Recipient								
EU001	BA	Fed. Min. of Agriculture, Water management and Forestry	Recipient								
EU001	LT	Min. of Env. Protection - Landscape & Biodiversity Dept.	Recipient								
EU001	LV	Min. of Env. Protection and Reg. Development - Env. Protection Dept.	Recipient								
EU001	HU	Min. of the Environment & Regional Policy, Dept. of N. P. & Forestry	Recipient								
EU001	EE	Ministry of Environment	Recipient								
EU001	CZ	Forest and Soil Protection Dept. Min. of the Environment	Recipient								
EU001	RO	Min. of Waters, Forests and Envir. Protection	Recipient								
EU001	SK	Min. of the Environment - Nature & Landscape Protection Dev. Dept.	Recipient								
EU001	AL	Committee of Environmental Protection, Min. of Health and Envir. Protection	Recipient								
EU001	EU	European Commission–Operational Serv. Phare	Donor								
EU001	PL	Dept. of State Forestry, Min. of Env. Protect., Natural Res. & Forestry	Recipient								
EU002	RU	Many institutions and industries in Baikal region	Recipient	Multilateral	Natural resources management in the Baikal water basin.	In planning	1996	1999	Capacity building	Policy/strategy	Know-how transfer
EU002	RU	Irkutsk Oblast Committee for Environment and Natural Resources	Recipient								

H3 Projects, International Organisations: *EU (continued)*

Project ID		Organization	Position	Cooperation	Title	Status	From/in	To	Type 1	Type 2	Type 3
EU002	RU	State Ecology Committee of the Republic of Buryatia	Recipient								
EU002	EU	The TACIS 1995 Action Programme, European Community	Donor								
EU003	EU	TACIS Action Programme - European Community	Donor	Multilateral	Forest management in north-west Russia	In planning	1996	1997	Capacity building	Policy/strategy	
EU003	RU	Karellesprom	Recipient								
EU003	RU	Karelian Ministry of Industry, Transport and Communication	Recipient								
EU003	RU	State Karelian Research Institute of Forest Industry	Recipient								
EU003	RU	Federal Forest Service of Russia	Recipient								
EU003	RU	Scientific Research and Information Centre for Forest Resources	Recipient								
EU003	RU	State Forestry Committee of the Republic of Karelia	Recipient								
FR001	EU	Commission Européene, DG III	Donor	Multilateral	Cooperation in mechanical wood-processing sector	Completed	1995	0	Seminar/workshop		
GB002	EU	European Community -- Polish Forest Development Programme	Donor	Multilateral	Polish Forest Development Programme	Completed	1995	0	Study tour		
GB003	EU	European Commission	Donor	Multilateral	Forestry Development Programme 1994	Completed	1994	0	Technical development		
GB004	EU	Commission of the European Communities, DGVIBII	Donor	Bilateral	European Community's Mission to the Russian Federation	Completed	1991	0	Study tour		
GB006	EU	Main Contractor, SODETEC	Donor	Multilateral	Technical Assistance to Ministry of Agriculture Project Management Unit in Latvia	Completed	1995	0	Policy/strategy		
GB018	EU	EU SHARE	Donor	Multilateral	Private forestry sector development in Latvia	Completed	1997	0	Study tour	Seminar/workshop	Education/training
HU001	EU	European Commission-- Phare	Donor	Multilateral	Business analysis on strategic review of the Hungarian State Forestry Portfolio	Completed	1995	0	Policy/strategy	Other (Strategic study)	
HU029	EU	Phare	Donor	Multilateral	Development of the forestry information system (HU–2001/IB/AG-02)	Ongoing	2002	2003	Capacity building	Institutional development	Technical development
HU030	EU	Phare	Donor	Multilateral	Wood Sector Study	Completed	1992	0	Policy/strategy		
HU031	EU	Phare	Donor	Multilateral	Wood Sector Study II	Completed	1993	0	Policy/strategy		
HU032	EU	Phare	Donor	Multilateral	Strategic Review (Forestry Portfolio Business Analysis)	Completed	1995	0	Policy/strategy		
LT003	EU	European Community -- Phare	Donor	Multilateral	Modernisation of Nursery of Dubrava Experimental Forest Enterprise	Completed	1996	1997	Technical development	Know-how transfer	

H3 Projects, International Organisations: *EU (continued)*

Project ID		Organization	Position	Cooperation	Title	Status	From/in	To	Type 1	Type 2	Type 3
LT005	EU	Phare	Donor	Bilateral	Dubrava nursery modernization project	Completed	1996	1997	Education/training		
LT028	EU	Phare PROJECT	Donor	Bilateral	Long-term technical training in nursery production			0	Education/training	Technical assistance	
LT031	EU	EU/Phare	Donor	Multilateral	Professional training of sawmill workers		1996	0	Education/training		
LV007	EU	European Community -- Phare	Donor	Multilateral	Technical assistance to the private forestry	In planning	1996	1997	Study tour	Seminar/workshop	Education/training
PL001	EU	Phare programme, European Commission	Donor	Multilateral	Forestry Development Programme	Completed	1995	1997	Scientific/research	Technical development	Know-how transfer
PL004	EU	Phare Programme, European Commission	Donor	Multilateral	Ecological and economic evaluation of the impact of nun moth control treatments on the forest environment	Ongoing	0	0	Seminar/workshop	Education/training	Scientific/research
PL009	EU	European Community	Donor	Multilateral	Genetic diversity of forest tree species in central Europe	Suggested	1996	1998	Scientific/research		
SI003	EU	European Commission -- Phare	Donor	Multilateral	Energy Conservation Strategy in Slovenia	Completed	1994	1995	Scientific/research		

H3 Projects, International Organisations: *EFI*

Project ID		Organization	Position	Cooperation	Title	Status	From/in	To	Type 1	Type 2	Type 3
EF001	SI		Recipient	Multilateral	Growth Trend of European Forests	Completed	1996	0	Scientific/research		
EF001	PL		Recipient								
EF001	RU		Recipient								
EF001	CZ		Recipient								
EF001	EF	European Forest Institute	Donor								
UA004	EF		Donor	Multilateral	Legal, administrative and policy strategies for securing sustainable development of the forest sector in Russia, Belarus and Ukrain (INTAS programme)	Completed	1996	1998	Policy/strategy	Institutional development	
UA009	EF	European Forest Institute	Donor	Multilateral	Scenario analysis of sustainable wood production under different forest management regimes (SCEFORMA) (INCO-Copernicus programme)	Ongoing	1998	2001	Education/training	Technical assistance	
UA013	EF	European Forest Institute	Donor		International conference "Challenges for Forestry in Central European Countries and Newly Independent States: breaking through in the EU".	In planning	0	0	Conference		
UA014	EF	European Forest Institute	Donor	Bilateral	Ukrainian Forestry Web-page for Forest Information Services Network for Europe (FINE)	In planning	2001	2003	Education/training		

H3 Projects, International Organisations: *European Investment Bank*

Project ID		Organization	Position	Cooperation	Title	Status	From/in	To	Type 1	Type 2	Type 3
PL007	IB	European Investment Bank, Luxembourg	Donor	Multilateral	Development of selected forestry branches and protection of ecosystems in National Parks in 1993-1997	Completed	1993	1997	Education/training	Technical development	Policy/strategy

H3 Projects, International Organisations: *FAO*

Project ID		Organization	Position	Cooperation	Title	Status	From/in	To	Type 1	Type 2	Type 3
AL002	FA	FAO	Donor	Multilateral	Integrated forestry management in Albania	Ongoing	0	0	Education/training	Technical development	Capacity building
AL003	FA	Food and Agriculture Organization of the United Nations	Donor	Multilateral	Projects under planning in cooperation with ICP Forest, ECE, World Bank, FAO, UNDP, UNEP, GEF, IUFRO, EBRD on the areas mentioned under the "contents"	In planning	0	0			
AM001	FA	Food and Agriculture Organization of the United Nations	Donor	Multilateral	Armenian forest sector development (FAO Technical Cooperation Programme ARM/4451/6612 (1994-1997) TCP)	Completed	1994	1997	Capacity building		
AT004	FA	FAO	Donor	Multilateral	FAO/Austria Seminar on the Economics and Management of Forest Operations for CITs	Completed	1994	0	Seminar/workshop		
CZ012	FA	IPGRI, Rome	Donor	Multilateral	Forest tree seed pathology meeting	Completed	1996	0	Seminar/workshop		
CZ034	FA	FAO	Donor		Strengthening of private and community forestry in Central and Eastern Europe	In planning	0	0			
FA001	FA	Forest Products Marketing Programme, FAO Regular Programme	Donor	Multilateral	Compendium of Computer-Based Databases of Relevance to Forest Products Marketing	Completed	1995	0	Capacity building		
FA001	AL		Recipient								
FA002	EC	UN Economic Commission for Europe	Donor	Multilateral	Development of marketing of sawnwood products in countries in transition to market economies	Completed	1995	0	Seminar/workshop	Capacity building	
FA002	EE		Donor								
FA002	FA	FAO	Donor								
FA002	FI		Donor								
FA003	AT	Ministry of Agriculture and Forestry	Donor	Multilateral	Seminar on Economics and Management of Forest Operations for CITs to market economies	Completed	1994	0	Seminar/workshop	Technical development	
FA004	AT	Ministry of Agriculture and Forestry	Donor	Multilateral	Follow up Seminar on Economics and Management of Forest Operations	Suggested	1997	0	Seminar/workshop		
FA005	FA	FAO	Donor	Multilateral	Control of nun moth and pine caterpillars.	Completed	1995	0	Education/training	Technical development	Know-how transfer
FA005	LT	Government of Lithuania	Recipient								
FA006	FA	FAO	Donor	Multilateral	Integrated Forest Management Project (legal component)	completed	1992	1993	Policy/strategy		
FA006	AL	General Directorate of Forestry	Recipient								
FA007	FA	FAO	Donor	Multilateral	GCP/ALB/OUI/ITA	completed	1993	0	Policy/strategy		
FA007	AL	General Directorate of Forestry	Recipient								
FA008	FA	FAO	Donor	Multilateral	TCP/ARM/4451 (Legal Component)	completed	1994	1995	Policy/strategy		
FA008	AM	Directorate General of Forests	Recipient								
HR001	FA	FAO	Donor	Multilateral	Coastel forest reconstruction and protection project	In planning	1996	2000	Scientific/research		
LT041	FA	FAO	Donor	Bilateral	Development of the private forestry sector in Lithuania	Completed	1998	2000	Seminar/workshop	Scientific/research	Technical development
LV001	FA	FAO	Donor	Multilateral	Research on grading rules and contract forms to be used in Latvia	Completed			Seminar/workshop	Scientific/research	Capacity building
SK001	FA	FAO	Donor	Multilateral	Institution-building, framework conditions and policy infrastructure for sustainable development of forestry	In planning	1996	0	Seminar/workshop		

Some facts about the Timber Committee

The Timber Committee is a principal subsidiary body of the UNECE (United Nations Economic Commission for Europe) based in Geneva. It constitutes a forum for cooperation and consultation between member countries on forestry, forest industry and forest product matters. All countries of Europe; the former USSR; United States, of America, Canada and Israel are members of the UNECE and participate in its work.

The UNECE Timber Committee shall, within the context of sustainable development, provide member countries with the information and services needed for policy- and decision-making regarding their forest and forest industry sector ("the sector"), including the trade and use of forest products and, when appropriate, formulate recommendations addressed to member Governments and interested organizations. To this end, it shall:

1. With the active participation of member countries, undertake short-, medium- and long-term analyses of developments in, and having an impact on, the sector, including those offering possibilities for the facilitation of international trade and for enhancing the protection of the environment;
2. In support of these analyses, collect, store and disseminate statistics relating to the sector, and carry out activities to improve their quality and comparability;
3. Provide the framework for cooperation e.g. by organizing seminars, workshops and ad hoc meetings and setting up time-limited ad hoc groups, for the exchange of economic, environmental and technical information between governments and other institutions of member countries that is needed for the development and implementation of policies leading to the sustainable development of the sector and to the protection of the environment in their respective countries;
4. Carry out tasks identified by the UNECE or the Timber Committee as being of priority, including the facilitation of subregional cooperation and activities in support of the economies in transition of central and eastern Europe and of the countries of the region that are developing from an economic point of view;
5. It should also keep under review its structure and priorities and cooperate with other international and intergovernmental organizations active in the sector, and in particular with the FAO (Food and Agriculture Organization of the United Nations) and its European Forestry Commission and with the ILO (International Labour Organisation), in order to ensure complementarity and to avoid duplication, thereby optimizing the use of resources.

More information about the Committee's work may be obtained by writing to:

Timber Section
Trade Development and Timber Division
UN Economic Commission for Europe
Palais des Nations
CH - 1211 Geneva 10, Switzerland
Fax: + 41 22 917 0041
E-mail: info.timber@unece.org
http://www.unece.org/trade/timber

UNECE/FAO Publications

Timber Bulletin Volume LV (2002)   ECE/TIM/BULL/2002/...
1. Forest Products Prices, 1998-2000
2. Forest Products Statistics, 1997-2001 (database since 1964 on website)
3. Forest Products Annual Market Review, 2001-2002
4. Forest Fire Statistics, 1999-2001
5. Forest Products Trade Flow Data, 1999-2000
6. Forest Products Markets in 2002 and Prospects for 2003

Geneva Timber and Forest Study Papers

Forest policies and institutions of Europe, 1998-2000   ECE/TIM/SP/19

Forest and Forest Products Country Profile: Russian Federation   ECE/TIM/SP/18
(Country profiles also exist on Albania, Armenia, Belarus, Bulgaria, former Czech and
Slovak Federal Republic, Estonia, Hungary, Lithuania, Poland, Romania,
Republic of Moldova, Slovenia and Ukraine)

Forest resources of Europe, CIS, North America, Australia, Japan and New Zealand   ECE/TIM/SP/17

State of European forests and forestry, 1999   ECE/TIM/SP/16

Non-wood goods and services of the forest   ECE/TIM/SP/15

The above series of sales publications and subscriptions are available through United Nations
Publications Offices as follows:

Orders from Africa, Europe and   *Orders from North America, Latin America and the*
Middle East should be sent to: *Caribbean, Asia and the Pacific should be sent to:*

Sales and Marketing Section, Room C-113   Sales and Marketing Section, Room DC2-853
United Nations   United Nations
Palais des Nations   2 United Nations Plaza
CH - 1211 Geneva 10, Switzerland   New York, N.Y. 10017, United States, of America
Fax: + 41 22 917 0027   Fax: + 1 212 963 3489
E-mail: unpubli@unog.ch   E-mail: publications@un.org

Web site: http://www.un.org/Pubs/sales.htm
* * * * *

Geneva Timber and Forest Discussion Papers *(original language only)*

Russian Federation Forest Sector Outlook Study	ECE/TIM/DP/27
Forest and Forest Products Country Profile: Georgia	ECE/TIM/DP/26
Forest certification update for the UNECE region, summer 2002	ECE/TIM/DP/25
Forecasts of economic growth in OECD and central and eastern European countries for the period 2000-2040	ECE/TIM/DP/24
Forest Certification update for the ECE Region, summer 2001	ECE/TIM/DP/23
Structural, Compositional and Functional Aspects of Forest Biodiversity in Europe	ECE/TIM/DP/22
Markets for secondary processed wood products, 1990-2000	ECE/TIM/DP/21
Forest certification update for the ECE Region, summer 2000	ECE/TIM/DP/20
Trade and environment issues in the forest and forest products sector	ECE/TIM/DP/19
Multiple use forestry	ECE/TIM/DP/18
Forest certification update for the ECE Region, summer 1999	ECE/TIM/DP/17
A summary of "The competitive climate for wood products and paper packaging: the factors causing substitution with emphasis on environmental promotions"	ECE/TIM/DP/16
Recycling, energy and market interactions	ECE/TIM/DP/15
The status of forest certification in the ECE region	ECE/TIM/DP/14
The role of women on forest properties in Haute-Savoie (France): Initial researches	ECE/TIM/DP/13
Interim report on the Implementation of Resolution H3 of the Helsinki Ministerial Conference on the protection of forests in Europe (Results of the second enquiry)	ECE/TIM/DP/12
Manual on acute forest damage	ECE/TIM/DP/7

International Forest Fire News *(two issues per year)*

Timber and Forest Information Series

Timber Committee Yearbook 2002	ECE/TIM/INF/9

The above series of publications may be requested free of charge through:

UNECE/FAO Timber Section
UNECE Trade Development and Timber Division
United Nations
Palais des Nations
CH - 1211 Geneva 10, Switzerland
Fax: + 41 22 917 0041
E-mail: info.timber@unece.org
Downloads are available at http://www.unece.org/trade/timber